MW00812010

The Reformation

A Captivating Guide to the Religious Revolution Sparked by Martin Luther and Its Impact on Christianity and the Western Church

Free Bonus from Captivating History (Available for a Limited time)

Hi History Lovers!

Now you have a chance to join our exclusive history list so you can get your first history ebook for free as well as discounts and a potential to get more history books for free! Simply visit the link below to join.

Captivatinghistory.com/ebook

Also, make sure to follow us on Facebook, Twitter and Youtube by searching for Captivating History.

Contents

Introduction: How the Reformation was Unleashed

In the early 1500s, Christianity was about as united as it would ever be. During this period, there were only two main branches of Christianity: the Catholicism of the West and the Orthodox Church of the East. East and West had split some 500 years prior due to some rather minor (yet consequential) doctrinal differences. It was only when the external threat of the advancing armies of Islam began the first of many attempts to batter down the doors of the Eastern Orthodox Church—whose seat was in Constantinople (modern-day Istanbul)—that the Catholic Church and the Orthodox Church attempted to mend fences.

Christendom launched Crusades from the West in an attempt to defend its eastern brothers, but in the end, the Eastern Orthodox Church, once headquartered in Asia Minor (modern-day Turkey), was overrun and subjugated to Islam. The remnants of Orthodox Christianity would survive, but in its tattered form, it would no longer pose a significant challenge to the Catholic Church as far as ideology. It wasn't until a man named Martin Luther began to question Catholic teachings in the early 1500s that new fractures in the church structure became visible.

Martin Luther became a Catholic priest in 1507. He was a dedicated member of the clergy but began to have serious misgivings with many aspects of official Catholic doctrine. The questions that began to arise in the heart of this lone monk led to him famously nailing his Ninety-five Theses to the doors of All Saints' Church (sometimes referred to as Castle Church) where he served. On October 31, 1517, about a decade after Luther's original ordination, he nailed his chief protests to the church doors for all to see.

The modern reader will note the date since it has since become associated with Halloween. Back in Luther's day, it was known as All Saints' Eve since the following day was November 1, which was (and still is) the Catholic holiday of All Saints' Day. All Saints' Day was also called All Hallows' Day in various quarters, and the night before would have been known as All Hallows' Eve, from which we get the modern variation of Halloween.

But as spooky as all that might sound, Luther, it seems, chose this date for no other reason than the fact that All Saints' Day (All Hallows' Day) was when many budding intellectuals of the church would meet. Knowing many people would be there on that day to discuss his treatises, he posted them on the door the day before so everyone would be sure to see them. The posting of these directives was not that unusual, either.

Many have likened his posting on the doors to someone posting notes on a bulletin board (or better yet, on Facebook) just to air an opinion. Martin Luther wasn't trying to do anything all that radical at the time—he was simply opening a dialogue and asking a few questions. Luther never intended to break up the Catholic Church or create opposing factions; he just sought to reform (hence the phrase Reformation) the Catholic Church from within. But little did he know the tidal wave of change he was about to unleash.

Chapter 1 – Martin's Ninety-Five Reasons for Reform

"From the beginning of my Reformation I have asked God to send me neither dreams, nor visions, nor angels, but to give me the right understanding of his Word, and the Holy Scriptures. For as long as I have God's Word, I know that I am walking in His way and that I shall not fall into any error or delusion."

- Martin Luther

Much has been made of the Ninety-five Theses (or theological propositions) that Martin Luther nailed up on the abbey door in 1517. But what did they entail? Despite the extraordinary social change they would spark, the theses themselves were not exactly radical in nature, and they focused on two main themes: Luther's belief that salvation was achieved by faith rather than works and Luther's insistence that Scripture should be the ultimate religious authority rather than clergy.

Of chief concern to Luther at the time was the fact that the church had been in the business of selling salvation to the masses through something called an indulgence. This practice allowed parishioners to literally give money to the Catholic Church in exchange for promises from the clergy to forgive them of sin and/or grant them passage from purgatory to Heaven. To understand the practice of indulgences, one must understand the teachings of the Catholic Church of this time period.

Catholics taught that sinners needed to undergo penance in this life and—often enough—also in the next. It was a common belief of the time that upon passing, most people didn't go immediately to Heaven or hell but rather to an in-between realm called purgatory. Since Luther's day, many Protestant groups have thoroughly ridiculed the idea of purgatory and have even gone so far as to say the Catholic Church made the whole thing up.

But although the word purgatory—a Latin word meaning to cleanse or purge—is most definitely not in Scripture, there is biblical mention of just such a place. The Bible did indeed often speak of an in-between or limbo realm where the saints "sleep." This place has been referred to by its Hebrew name of Sheol. The original Greek of the New Testament used the Greek word for Sheol, which is Hades, to describe the same exact place. The same realm has also come through translation as "paradise," or even "Abraham's Bosom."

It can be confusing to have such pleasant-sounding names as "paradise" and "Abraham's Bosom" for a place Catholic's called purgatory. Also of confusion is the use of the Greek word "Hades," which most people probably associate with the Western concept of hell, but hell and Hades are two different concepts. While hell is defined as a place of torment, Hades is simply the underworld abode of the dead.

The actual Greek term for a place of torment akin to our common notion of hell is the word "Tartarus." In the Greek translation of the New Testament, the word "Tartarus" only appears one time when the Apostle Peter is describing the final destination of the fallen angels who disobeyed God. The choice of this word is interesting because, in Greek mythology, Tartarus is the place where the Titans were imprisoned. If you read up on Greek myths and compare them with the biblical stories of the fallen angels/watchers/Nephilim, the parallels are rather stunning.

It makes one wonder, was the word "Tartarus" chosen out of convenience, or was it indeed referring to the same exact place? Did the Apostle Peter see some sort of similarity between the popular Greek tales of the Titans and the fallen angels? At any rate, as it pertains to Sheol, Hades, paradise, and Abraham's Bosom—all these realms spoken of in the Bible, regardless of what they are called, fulfill the same purpose of the Catholic purgatory. They are neither Heaven nor hell, but merely a place where transitory souls are temporarily holed up.

These concepts are complex, and save for theologians who spend years studying them in- depth, most Christians probably do not know much about them. But, as strange as they may sound to the casual observer, these concepts are based on Scripture. Early Christians believed that before Jesus came to Earth and died on the cross, all the Old Testament saints (such as Abraham) were denied access to Heaven, yet God certainly wasn't going to send them to hell, so instead, they were kept in an in-between plane of existence—hence Abraham's bosom, paradise, purgatory, Sheol, or whatever you wish to call it.

According to this notion, Jesus himself, after being crucified, descended down into this netherworld to "set the captives free." Today, preachers are more likely to use this as an allegory to deliver a feel-good message to the masses about how Jesus liberates those in bondage to things such as alcohol or some other vice. There is certainly nothing wrong with that, but the expression has a literal interpretation, as well. The three days between Christ's crucifixion and resurrection is a dramatic part of New Testament Scripture that is often overlooked, but according to the Bible, he wasn't idle.

Scripture tells us that immediately after being killed on the cross, Jesus went straight to paradise/purgatory and quite literally "led captivity captive" by rescuing the Old Testament saints who were being held in Sheol. It was only after this mission was complete that Jesus Christ was physically resurrected from the dead and emerged from the tomb—back from the dead and back from that underworld realm of purgatory called Sheol/Hades.

According to the Bible, in the three days prior to his resurrection, Jesus was on a spiritual mission to set souls who had long been stuck in a purgatory limbo free. He did not enter Heaven until his physical resurrection and eventual ascension in what Christians refer to as his "glorified" or "immortal/incorruptible" body—a state of being that Christians believe they, too, will be transformed into in the "twinkling of an eye" when the "last trumpet sounds."

The idea that Jesus went to paradise first, *before* resurrection and ascension, is also supported by a remark Jesus made to the thief on the cross: "This day you will be with me in paradise." He didn't say Heaven but specifically said "paradise," which is another word for Sheol/Abraham's Bosom/Hades—you get the point.

This is a lot to unpack, but understanding such things is essential to understanding why Catholics spoke of an in-between realm called purgatory. Despite misinformation and the insinuation that purgatory is simply nonsense someone made up, the concept of purgatory is one that is grounded in Scripture.

At any rate, Catholics greatly expanded upon all of this and eventually came to believe that one could lessen the time spent in purgatory by paying indulgences to priests—or even help dead relatives believed to be in purgatory by paying on their behalf. As for Martin Luther, it is said that he would later drop much of his previous belief in purgatory, but at the time he nailed his Ninety-five Theses to the door, he wasn't so much against the notion of purgatory itself as the idea that one could pay their way out of it.

As corrupt as such a bargain might seem at first glance, the act of paying money or "alms" on behalf of a deceased loved one wasn't simply a scheme hatched by the Catholic Church. Just like purgatory, it was derived from Scripture. The concept of indulgences stems from Maccabees—a book which, coincidentally enough, is excluded from most Protestant Bibles. The concept of paying a sacrificial amount of money for the souls of the departed comes from an account of Judas Maccabeus advising his followers to pay alms for some of his warriors who had perished in battle.

These warriors were found to have amulets around their necks that were considered profane and in reverence to pagan gods. It was for the atonement of the acts of these dead men that Judas requested all his followers to offer up alms. Or, as 2 Maccabees 42-45 tells us, "The noble Judas called on the people to keep themselves free from sin, for they had seen with their own eyes what had happened to the fallen because of their sin. He levied a contribution from each man and sent the total of two thousand silver drachmas to Jerusalem for a sin offering—a fit and proper act in which he took due account of the resurrection. For if he had not been expecting the fallen to rise again, it would have been foolish and superfluous to pray for the dead. But since he had in view the wonderful reward reserved for those who die a godly death, his purpose was a holy and pious one. And this was why he offered an atoning sacrifice to free the dead from their sin."

Maccabees clearly gives an example of praying for the dead and paying alms (an indulgence) for them in the hopes that this atoning sacrifice would "free the dead from their sin." Protestant Bibles would choose not to include the Book of Maccabees. Roman Catholic priests however, could readily point to this one Scripture as part of their reasoning behind allowing indulgences to be made for those offering alms for the dearly departed.

As it pertains to Martin Luther's reasons for nailing his Ninety-five Theses to the church doors on October 31, 1517, he was primarily critical of what he saw as blatant abuses of the practice. Luther was particularly irked by priests who had used the sales of indulgences to fund building projects. In Luther's day, the acquisition of indulgences had become so thoroughly commercialized that, at one point, a

Dominican friar by the name of Johan Tetzel had created his own advertising jingle to get proceeds. The crafty friar was allegedly fond of proclaiming, "As soon as the coin in the coffer rings, a soul from purgatory to heaven springs!"

Luther believed that such malfeasance was corrupting to the clergy just as much as it was to the congregation since it made the public think they could avoid true repentance and simply pay their way into Heaven instead. Martin Luther decisively condemned such practices in Thesis 32 of his Ninety-five Theses, which stated, "Those who believe that they can be certain of their salvation because they have indulgence letters will be eternally damned, together with their teachers." In Thesis 43, he then further clarified this belief when he declared, "Christians are to be taught that he who gives to the poor or lends to the needy does a better deed than he who buys indulgences."

He also decisively rebuked the Church's practice of using indulgence money to fund building projects. In Thesis 50, Luther had steadfastly proclaimed, "Christians are to be taught that if the pope knew the exactions of the indulgence preachers, he would rather that the basilica of St. Peter were burned to ashes than built up with the skin, flesh, and bones of his sheep."

It's important to note that while Luther excoriated clergy, whom he called "indulgence preachers," he still managed to hold the pope himself blameless. When Luther nailed his Ninety-five Theses to those church doors, he still believed that the pope was not aware of what lower-level clergy (most especially the likes of Johan Tetzel) were doing.

Instead, Martin Luther insisted that the pope was ignorant of such things, and if he only knew, "he would rather that the basilica of St. Peter were burned to ashes than built up with the skin, flesh, and bones of his sheep." As you can see, at this point in his own personal evolution of thought, Luther was willing to give the pope in faraway Rome the benefit of the doubt—his views, however, would soon change.

Chapter 2 – Luther Gets Labeled a Heretic

"Unless I am convicted by Scripture and plain reason, I do not accept the authority of popes and councils, for they have contradicted each other. My conscience is captive to the Word of God. I cannot and will not recant anything, for to go against conscience is neither right nor safe. Here I stand, I cannot do otherwise. God help me. Amen."

- Martin Luther

In the immediate aftermath of Martin Luther nailing his Ninety-five Theses to the doors of Wittenberg's Castle Church, his religious tracts made the rounds and were circulated freely. Luther's words seemed to resonate with the German masses, who were largely disenchanted with Rome's grip over local church affairs. Luther's daring rebukes stirred up their own skepticism of papal authority. But, by the time copies of Luther's theses reached Rome itself, the reaction was initially one of indifference.

Roman clergy believed that Luther's main argument was against the Dominican order of friars such as Johan Tetzel, an order that was often at odds with the Augustinian order to which Martin Luther belonged. Luther did indeed criticize Tetzel and seemed to shield the pope himself from blame, merely pointing out the perceived abuses of the clergy under his authority. Luther, in fact, had professed his belief that if the pope only knew of the abuses that were occurring, he was certain to put a stop to it.

Martin Luther presented himself as a faithful priest who had a disagreement with how other priests conducted themselves, so it's understandable why Roman Catholic authorities initially shrugged off the whole thing as a petty squabble between monks. Yet, as the debate continued to rage and more voices became involved in the drama, the Vatican couldn't help but take notice.

By 1518, Luther's words were being printed in both Latin and German, and although he never gained a copyright or royalties from his work, his tracts had become something of a best seller. Soon, everyone was talking about the ideas of this previously unknown and obscure Augustinian monk. It was while riding this wave of interest that Luther made his way to the University of Heidelberg in April of 1518 to speak freely to a live audience.

Even at this point, there was concern over Luther's personal security since some people had already shown strong opposition to his teachings. Nevertheless, the local German authority—the Elector of Saxony, Frederick the Wise—granted Luther a letter guaranteeing safe passage should anyone try to intercept him. In the meantime, Luther did not have the intention of stirring up debate during this visit. His original plans were to deliver a lecture over the merits of Saint Augustine's theology. As an Augustinian monk himself, this was certainly some well-trod territory.

Yet, for those who had gathered, the main draw was not to hear about St. Augustine, but rather the growing controversy over Luther's Ninety-five Theses. They especially wanted to hear Luther reference his recent arguments against the practice of indulgences. And, while Luther did not delve too deeply into his ideas on indulgences, he did touch on other matters that would be extremely important to the coming Reformation. He spoke of his views on the righteousness of faith through Christ and expounded on his notion of the utter impotence of human beings to achieve their own salvation.

Luther's lecture at Heidelberg was well received and a great success, rendering him almost a local celebrity. But as his fame grew, so did his opposition. By the summer of 1518, he was being assailed by one of the top Catholic minds in the region—John Eck. Eck took direct issue with Luther's Ninety-five Theses and wrote his own opposition piece, titled "Obelisks." Here, Eck railed against Luther and attempted to tear apart his arguments.

Luther was initially stunned by the onslaught, never imagining that someone like Eck could take such an issue with his mere questioning of a practice such as indulgences. Luther soon got over his shock, however, and went on the offensive. Holding nothing back, he picked up his pen and unleashed upon his opponent in the bombastic manner that would make him famous. At one point, he famously declared Eck to be behaving like nothing more than "an irritated prostitute" that vomits up terrible curses and oaths.

With rhetoric like this, there was no going back. A line had been drawn in the sand, and as it pertained to Luther, either you loved the man or you thought he was an abominable heretic. Soon enough, even faraway Rome was setting things in motion to silence this troublesome monk. On August 7, 1518, Luther was stunned to receive official correspondence from the Vatican, which proclaimed that his Ninety-five Theses were deemed heretical. As such, Luther was asked to report to Rome to answer for his errors.

This was a dangerous prospect for Luther, however, since it meant he would have to leave his relatively safe German backyard and present himself in Rome at the complete mercy of the Vatican—an institution which, in those days, was usually not too kind to those whom it believed to be leading the flock astray. As it were, in fact, there were already a few schemes afoot to forcibly arrest Luther. If possible, the German Augustinians were instructed to lay hold of Luther and "send him to Rome bound hand and foot in chains."

A sign of the weakening hold of Rome was apparent, however, in the fact that this never occurred. During Luther's day, the so-called "Holy Roman Empire" was the real powerhouse. And, although the spiritual center of the Holy Roman Empire was meant to be in Rome, the political center of the Holy Roman Empire of Luther's time was in the German principalities of Central Europe. (To clear up any confusion, it's important to note that "Germany" as we know it today had yet to be born. Sure, there were Germanic peoples who spoke German, of which Martin Luther himself was a part, but the modern nation-state of Germany would not come about until 1871.) During Luther's day, what we now call Germany was a part of the Holy Roman Empire, which at that time encompassed what is now modern-day Germany, Austria, Switzerland, part of France, part of Italy, and part of Poland. Accordingly, instead of being sent to Rome, Luther was instead given the option of going to the imperial parliament of the German city of Augsburg in October of 1518.

Here Luther was personally questioned by the papal legate of Augsburg, a fellow by the name of Cardinal Cajetan, over the course of three days. It was Cardinal Cajetan who repeatedly insisted that Luther was wrong and demanded that he correct his "errors" over the practice of indulgences and his views on the extent of papal authority. Luther refused, however, and shortly thereafter, Cardinal Cajetan labeled Luther a heretic, and requested the German authorities either "send him to Rome or chase him from Saxony."

Luther himself knew that his freedom was very much in jeopardy at this point, and as such, quickly left Augsburg for safer ground in northern Germany. Again, it is important to consider the political situation in the region at that time. The land we more commonly call Germany, was a part of the Holy Roman Empire. In 1518, this empire was ruled by the Holy Roman Emperor, Maximilian I. As fate would have it, Maximilian abruptly passed away in January of 1519. This left his grandson, Charles V, as his successor.

Charles could not become the official ruler of the HRE (Holy Roman Empire) until he was chosen by the seven imperial electors— yes, interestingly, the Holy Roman Emperor was ultimately chosen by an "electoral college." In much the same manner as a United States president is chosen by electors scattered throughout fifty states, the Holy Roman Emperor was put in power by the seven electors of the HRE, who were also in charge of various principalities in the region.

The electors would designate the next monarchical candidate as the emperor-elect before final confirmation was given by the pope. All this might indeed sound almost amusing to an American reader due to its similarities to the United States electoral college, electors, and the concept of having a president-elect until the new leader is officially confirmed. But, as it turns out, the Founding Fathers of America borrowed many of their ideas from other places and times; the concept of the electoral college was one such notion they grafted into the US constitution.

At any rate, the electors represented important territories such as Cologne, Mainz, Trier, Saxony, Palatine of the Rhine, Margrave of Brandenburg, and Bohemia. These regions made up what was known as the "Imperial Diet," which was considered a deliberative body of the Holy Roman Empire. It was in this deliberative forum that much of Luther's later debates would take place.

At the time of Maximilian's death, Luther was living under the jurisdiction of the Elector of Saxony, the German Prince Frederick III. Frederick was a conservative when it came to religion, but he also happened to be the founder of Wittenberg and a stalwart champion of its resident theologian—Martin Luther. Luther had a great protector in the form of Frederick III, and as such, Rome had to tread cautiously when dealing with him. They could call him a heretic, but lest the pope alienate one of the electors of the HRE, Rome could not directly intervene.

Chapter 3 – Martin Luther Gets Ready for Battle

"The world doesn't want to be punished. It wants to remain in darkness. It doesn't want to be told that what it believes is false. If you also don't want to be corrected, then you might as well leave the church and spend your time at the bar and brothel. But if you want to be saved and remember that there's another life after this one you must accept correction."

-    Martin Luther

Either divine providence or just plain old good luck created some rather fortuitous circumstances for Martin Luther in 1519. It was that year that Holy Roman Emperor Maximillian perished, and the contest began for a new emperor to be declared by the HRE's electoral college. In the meantime, the mini-ruler of the place Luther resided—the Elector of Saxony, Prince Frederick III—was a man who was determined to keep the realm under his control and entirely free from Roman interference.

The University of Wittenberg in which Luther taught was also a site of extreme importance for the region, and Luther was a valuable member of the faculty. As such, Frederick III was not about to allow power players in Rome to simply snatch Luther up and take him away. Instead, Frederick remained adamant that Luther, as a German theologian, needed to be tried by a German court.

Pope Leo X, on the other hand, was not willing to press his luck on the matter since he was dependent upon Elector Frederick when it came to the electoral vote. Luther, in the meantime, was dependent on this valuable elector's protection. It was with this assurance that he continued to debate Catholic clergy.

One of the most famous of these debates took place in June of 1519 when Luther made his way to Leipzig to face off with Johann Eck, a faithful member of the Roman Catholic Church. Eck was considered an intelligent and esteemed theologian among his peers, but Luther referred to him as nothing more than a "little glory-hungry beast." In his debate with Eck, Luther stressed that Christian doctrine should not be directed by the supposed infallibility of the pope, but rather the Bible, or as Luther put it, "the infallible word of God."

Eck was rather belligerent in his attempts to rebuff Luther's assertions but dogmatically insisted that it was heresy to question allegiance to the pope. Luther, however, was quick to point out that the early church (as in the days of the apostles and shortly thereafter) had no papal authority to follow, and the Greek Orthodox Church, which had parted ways with the Catholic Church since the Great Schism, was no longer following directives from the pope, either. Luther used these two precedents to bolster his claim that the pope should not be the beat-all, end-all authority in matters of faith.

Luther had not yet officially broken with the pope; he was just stressing the need to be able to question papal directives. Even so, in more private communications, Luther had gone so far as to openly speculate that perhaps the pope was "the Antichrist himself." Luther was not quite prepared for the masterful performance that seasoned debater Johann Eck put on. Luther's delivery was rushed, and he is said to have seemed agitated and even a little unhinged throughout the engagement.

The audience also didn't seem too pleased when Luther began to suggest that purgatory might not be scriptural after all—even though theologians like Eck were more than ready to point to specific Scriptures to bolster their interpretation. But the moment that Eck truly let loose on Luther was when he mentioned John Huss, a reformer that lived some 100 years prior and was burned at the stake for his beliefs. Eck was probably bringing up Huss to frighten Luther and remind him of what might possibly be in store for him if he persisted.

Luther refused to back down, however, and remarked that Huss very well could have been right in some of his assertions. One can imagine the gasp let out by those in attendance. This was the trap that Eck had laid for Luther, and he didn't hesitate to take advantage of it. As soon as he had Luther identifying with a confirmed heretic, it was easy for Eck to paint Luther as one and the same.

It was soon after his engagement with Johann Eck that the local universities began to move against Luther, with many of them burning his writings and making pronouncements against him. But Martin Luther proved himself to be just as shrewd of a politician as he was a theologian. While the clergy were being encouraged to condemn Luther, he was contacting all the major political players in the region and stoking their sense of nationalism, in opposition to what was perceived as foreign interference.

Yes, as much as Martin Luther was a religious reformer, in many ways, he was also a German nationalist who decried foreign interference from Rome. As such, he didn't hesitate to play upon the German authorities' independent streak in encouraging them to aid him in his reformation of the church. He informed them that the Bible calls all Christians to act and made it clear that they did not need to wait for papal directives from Rome to do so.

As one might imagine, the Catholic Church would not take such things kindly. By the following summer of 1520, the pope issued a papal bull (official edict) in which the philosophies of Martin Luther were labeled a "poisonous virus." The pope highlighted what he perceived to be forty different errors in Martin Luther's ideology and gave Luther sixty days to present himself to the Vatican to answer to these supposed errors or risk being excommunicated from the church.

Martin Luther was not shaken or in any way deterred, however. Sixty days later, rather than report to Rome, Luther and his followers lit a bonfire in which they burned Roman Catholic literature—including the very papal bull that had been sent to him. As Luther cast the papal bull into the fire, he is said to have declared, regarding the pope, "Because you have confounded the truth of God, today the Lord confounds you. Into the fire with you!"

The pope finally answered this challenge by issuing another papal bull on January 3, 1521, which officially excommunicated Martin Luther, as well as those who followed him. He was accused of having a depraved mind and of being the leader of a "pernicious and heretical sect." In the past, such a condemnation would have brought those guilty of the trespasses to Rome to face punishment, but Luther continued to be protected by the local ruler, Frederick III.

Instead of being extradited to Rome, Luther was asked to show up at the next scheduled meeting of the Imperial Diet, which was set to take place in a town called Worms. This gathering would be presided over by the newly-elected Holy Roman Emperor, Charles V. This guaranteed Luther safe passage to the forum, but there was still the risk that he would be clandestinely seized by forces working for the Vatican and hauled off to face the pope.

Martin Luther himself knew full well the risk he was taking by going to the Diet of Worms, but he decided that he had to hold firm regardless. He voiced his sentiment to a close confidant of his at the time by stating, "If God does not want to preserve me, then my head is of slight importance compared with Christ." Luther figured that if God wished for him and his work to continue, his safety would be assured. If not, then it would not be of much importance in the long run. Arming himself with nothing more than his faith, Martin Luther was ready for battle.

Chapter 4 – The Diet of Worms and the War of Words

"We must make a great difference between God's Word and the word of man. A man's word is a little sound, that flies into the air, and soon vanishes. But the Word of God is greater than heaven and Earth. Yea, greater than death and hell. For it forms part of the power of God, and endures everlastingly."

- Martin Luther

Prior to being summoned to present himself before the Imperial Diet of Worms for questioning, Martin Luther's safety had been assured by his local benefactor, the Elector of Saxony. He was nominally safe in the German states of the Holy Roman Empire, but making his way to Worms still presented some risk, a fact that was signaled by the Holy Roman Emperor ordering the seizure of certain texts Luther had written. The new emperor was apparently trying to play it safe lest the pope think he was being friendly with a known heretic.

Luther appeared before the Diet on April 17, 1521. The power of Luther's growing celebrity was once again proven at this event. It's said that the population of the city of Worms doubled due to the rush of spectators who simply wished to get a glimpse of the man who had stirred up so much controversy.

Unlike his other notorious engagements, however, Luther was not there to debate. During the Diet of Worms, Luther was expected to only speak when directly asked a question. When presented with his own written works, for example, he was asked, "Are these your books?" And when Luther confirmed that they were, he was then asked if he wished to renounce what he had written—which, of course, Luther refused to do.

Luther knew that this was coming and, in fact, had joked with one of his friends beforehand by remarking, "This shall be my recantation at Worms: 'Previously I said the pope is the vicar of Christ. I recant. Now I say the pope is the adversary of Christ and the apostle of the Devil.'" In other words, rather than apologizing and recanting his previous remarks, Luther intended to double down even further.

Despite his bombast before his arrival, once he was seated before high-ranking members of the clergy, Luther seemed to momentarily lose his nerve. In a shaky, morose sounding voice, Luther asked if he could be given a little while to consider the consequences. Ecken and his colleagues then discussed the matter, and though it was against Ecken's better judgment, they reached the consensus that Luther would be given some time to think it over. In fact, they gave him a whole day, dismissing the monk and instructing him to return the following day. Luther was at a crossroads and grappling with his own will. The future of the Reformation, in the meantime, would depend on what he decided to do next. After being allowed to sleep on it, Luther did indeed return to the diet the next day, on April 18. This time, he was taken to a much larger room that allowed for a bigger crowd to be assembled to watch the main event. Luther was once again subjected to several rounds of questioning, but he was notably calmer this time and seemed to be much better prepared for the occasion. He held fast to his previous teachings, explaining that his work typically fell into three categories. One category was his commentary on Scripture, another his critique of what he perceived to be errors of the Vatican, and the third was his writings directed at those who debated his theology.

The most ground Luther would give was in admitting that some of his treatises that criticized individual members of the clergy may have gone a little too far in their vitriolic nature. But although his choice of words could be a bit sensational at times, he maintained that their intention was good and the works themselves should not be banned. Luther stood by his work, although he acknowledged his own flawed character traits, admitting, "I do not set myself up as a saint."

Luther maintained that he only used such over-the-top language to get his point across when he felt that others needed to be corrected. He furthermore insisted that he was unable to recant of his previous writings because he truly believed the pope needed to be corrected of his idolatry and tyranny. He then challenged his interrogators by suggesting that if they could prove his writings contradicted Scripture, he would be the first to "cast them into the flames."

The main purpose of this supposed trial, however, was not so much to understand Luther's beliefs as it was to get him to recant from them. His interrogators were not in the least impressed by his interpretation of Scripture or philosophy. Ecken, weary of Luther's long replies, at one point bluntly informed him that "he doubted Luther had somehow discovered something new in Christianity after fifteen centuries of history."

As confrontational as this whole episode was, towards the end of his interrogation, Luther tried to strike a more conciliatory tone by suggesting that he welcomed the vigorous discussion that his words had caused. He declared, "I must say that for me it is a joyful spectacle to see that passions and conflicts arise over the Word of God. For that is how the Word of God works! As the Lord Jesus said, 'I came to send not peace, but a sword.'" Luther's words rubbed his interrogator, Johann von der Ecken, the wrong way, however, and Ecken even accused Luther of arrogant insolence in his remarks.

Ecken then demanded once again that Luther state whether he intended to recant or stand by his claims. After a moment, Luther issued his response. In words that would go down in history, he steadfastly declared, "Unless I am convicted by Scripture and plain reason—I do not accept the authority of popes and councils, for they have contradicted each other—my conscience is captive to the Word of God. I cannot and I will not recant anything, for to go against conscience is neither right nor safe. Here I stand. I cannot do otherwise. God help me. Amen."

Ecken slammed Luther as one who was attempting to pretend that he was wiser than all the teachers of the church and had a better knowledge of the Bible than they. Holy Roman Emperor Charles was not too impressed, either. Although he did indeed ensure Luther safe passage from the forum, the emperor made his displeasure known. He issued an official edict in which he declared that Luther was to be "held in detestation as a limb severed from the Church of God, the author of a pernicious schism, a manifest and obstinate heretic."

Such a decree put Luther in a very precarious position since just about anyone on the street willing to act out against him would now seem to have the full backing of not only the Catholic Church but also the Holy Roman Emperor. The Roman Emperor had guaranteed Luther safe passage, so he could not simply have one of his troops kill Luther, but nothing would stop a random passerby from doing the dirty work for him. Therefore, upon leaving the Diet of Worms, Luther had to be on guard lest he was seized by some Catholic zealot hell-bent on exacting vengeance for the pope.

Luther would not be assaulted during his trip back to Wittenberg. Instead, he would be intercepted by emissaries of his protector, the Elector of Saxony. These men staged a kidnapping to bring Luther directly under their protective custody. Luther was held at Wartburg (German for "Watch Tower") Castle, where under the care of his powerful friend, he set to work translating the Bible into German—a translation in which Luther would later relegate traditional books he felt were less inspired, such as the book of James, Hebrews, and even the prophetic text of Revelation, to an appendix in the back.

Most important for the movement, however, was his decision to do away with Old Testament books such as the book of Maccabees, since it was from this book that the Catholic Church pointed to verses that seemed to justify their concepts of both purgatory and indulgences. Later Protestant Bibles would continue to omit Maccabees but would go against Luther's directive to minimize the importance of books such as James, Hebrews, and Revelation, allowing them to remain intact.

Holed up in Warburg Castle, Martin Luther grew his hair out, dressed as a knight, and went by the name of "Junker Jorg," or "Knight George." Meanwhile, back at Wittenberg University, Luther's followers were attempting to continue the reform that Luther had begun. Leading this group of young scholars was a young man by the name of Philipp Melanchthon.

Philipp tried to hold his own in the Reformation movement, but he was eventually too overwhelmed by the more conservative forces at work and was effectively silenced. But thankfully for the movement, one of Philipp's colleagues, a certain Professor Andreas Karlstadt, mustered up the fortitude to continue. It was Karlstadt that started taking some of Luther's ideas and putting them into practice, such as refraining from making use of the traditional vestments of a priest when conducting mass.

Karlstadt would also later (and rather dramatically) put another of Martin Luther's objections to Catholic tradition to practice by taking back his vow of celibacy and marrying a young woman by the name of Anna von Mochau, whom he wed in January of 1522. Although still a celibate monk himself at the time, Luther did indeed object to the idea that priests needed to be celibate. Luther had declared that such man-made vows were a "vain attempt to win salvation" and were ultimately illegitimate and false.

With his marriage to Anna von Mochau, Karlstadt showed that he wholeheartedly agreed with Luther's assessment. Martin Luther himself would eventually get married, as well. One can understand later criticisms of Luther from the Catholic Church by those who felt that he was simply some lustful monk that wanted to get married. But this, of course, glosses over the fundamental flaws that Luther saw in church teaching at the time. Luther didn't want to just break tradition and do as he pleased—he had some serious issues with the Catholic Church's teachings.

Although Luther initially just wanted to reform the Catholic Church, the Reformation would take on a militant shape that he could hardly have envisioned. Early in his stay at Castle Wartburg, he heard of various doctrinal splits and sects coming into existence. The theological clashes were creating stress not only for clergy but also for local political leadership since the turmoil of pro-Reformation and anti-Reformation sects was often so volatile it verged on violence.

Martin Luther's personal protector, Prince Frederick, feared that the situation would become too chaotic for him to maintain governance. Luther even expressed alarm at what was transpiring. At one point, he wrote down his thoughts, stating, "I have been waiting for Satan to attack this sensitive spot—but he decided not to make use of the papists. Now he is making efforts in and among us evangelicals to produce the worst conceivable schism. May Christ quickly trample him under his feet."

Martin Luther seemed to believe that the chaotic forces he helped to unleash were somehow of satanic influence. Hearing of the turmoil, Luther could no longer stand idly by, and despite the risk to his own personal wellbeing, he left his exile in Castle Wartburg and made his way back to Wittenberg University in the spring of 1522.

Upon his return to Wittenberg, Luther set about trying to restore some semblance of peace. He delivered several sermons, referred to as his "Invocavit Sermons," named as such since they began on Invocate Sunday, the first Sunday of Lent. In Luther's remarks, he made it clear he believed that some of his followers were taking things too far. He stressed that reform needed to be a gradual, slow process—not outright revolutionary change. Luther maintained that Christians needed to be slowly guided out of the old ways of the church. As he put it, "No one should be dragged to them [the Catholic Church] or away from them by the hair, for I can drive no man to heaven or beat him into it with a club."

At this time, Luther found himself at odds with his former ally Karlstadt, who he immediately banned from the pulpit and denounced as a "rebellious, murderous, seditious spirit." Karlstadt seems to have taken the reforms of Luther too far and too fast for its author to handle. Karlstadt, nonplussed by Luther's reaction, quickly labeled Luther as nothing more than a half-hearted reformer who was no better than the pope.

Luther also took issue with certain reforms that Karlstadt was attempting to make. Luther especially despised Karlstadt's decision to do away with infant baptism. Luther had learned long ago as an Augustinian monk that all are born with the stain of original sin and believed that infant baptism was necessary to remove it. Luther would cling to this belief for the rest of his life, and as it pertained to at least this ancient practice of the church, he defied any reformer who attempted to omit it.

Martin Luther fought Karlstadt tooth and nail over this and many other issues. At the cost of a former friend and ally, Luther reestablished himself as the leader of the movement. Under Luther's much more steady hand, the situation in Wittenberg was once again under control. But soon enough, the tremors of the Reformation would break through new ground further afield, and even the skillful oratory of Martin Luther would not be able to so easily constrain it.

In Switzerland, for example, a prominent rival had arisen in the form of a Swiss preacher named Huldrych Zwingli. It was in 1522, during Lent, that Zwingli bucked tradition in a big way by simply hosting a gathering in which parishioners ate sausage. This might sound almost humorous today, but at the time, it was a big deal since it broke the traditional stipulation of not eating meat prior to Easter.

Reformers like Zwingli tapped into the popular local sentiment in which people (Germanic peoples, especially) wished to override some of the practice forced on them by the Roman Catholic Church and bring back local cultural traditions. They were going to eat sausage whether the Pope condemned them for it or not. Luther was no doubt the inspiration for this sudden defiance.

Another direct offshoot of the Reformation Luther had begun was a local preacher by the name of Thomas Müntzer. Müntzer had been a follower of Luther who took up an early interest in his teachings. In fact, it was Luther who had installed Thomas Müntzer as a priest at Zwickau in 1520. Thomas wished to move at a much faster pace than Luther, however, and he consequently found himself at odds with both Luther and the Catholic Church.

Due to the discord that had emerged, it wasn't long before Thomas Müntzer turned his back on Luther altogether. He began to criticize Luther for not accepting his prophetic vision. Feeling that Luther was a bit too comfortable to be the revolutionary religious leader the people needed, Müntzer began to deride Martin Luther, calling him "Brother Fattened Swine" and "Brother Soft Life."

Not only that, Müntzer began to advocate the violent overthrow of those whom he felt were not doing enough to reform the Catholic Church. At one point, Thomas Müntzer unabashedly declared, "The angels who sharpen their sickles for the cutting are the earnest servants of God who fulfill the zeal of divine wisdom." It was this one radical reformer—Thomas Müntzer— and his militancy that would eventually lead to an all-out war.

Chapter 5 – The Reformation Heats Up

"If anyone attempted to rule the world by the gospel and to abolish all temporal law and sword on the plea all are baptized and Christian, and that according to the gospel, there shall be among them no law or sword—or need for either—pray tell me, friend, what would he be doing? He would be loosing the ropes and chains of the savage wild beasts and letting them bite and mangle everyone, meanwhile insisting that they were harmless, tame, and gentle creatures; but I would have the proof in my wounds. Just so would the wicked under the name of Christian abuse evangelical freedom, carry on their rascality, and insist that they were Christians subject neither to law nor sword, as some are already raving and ranting."

- Martin Luther

The radical reformer, Thomas Müntzer, wished to bring change far faster than Martin Luther would have liked. The former pupil slammed Luther as being soft and demanded that he develop a more aggressive stance against Catholic teaching. It was in castigation of this supposed softness that Müntzer wrote up the tract "A Highly Provoked Defense and Answer to the Spiritless, Soft-living Flesh at Wittenberg who Has Most Lamentably Befouled Pitiable Christianity in a Perverted Way by His Theft of Holy Scripture."

Thomas Müntzer, on the other hand, advocated open violence and destruction that led to widescale rioting in which both churches and clergy were attacked. In 1524, Müntzer found his way to the city of Mühlhausen in the region of Thuringia, where he met up with a fellow zealous reformer by the name of Heinrich Pfeiffer and crafted a list of demands called the "Eleven Mühlhausen Articles," in which the pair tried to pressure local governance to better match their interpretation of what they called biblical truth.

Müntzer's pushes for revolutionary reform would eventually lead to the terrible infighting of 1525, known as the Peasants' War. The Peasants' War was a grassroots uprising of the peasant class against not only the Catholic Church but also the entire landed gentry—it was just as much an economic/political war as it was a religious one. The downtrodden peasants were trying to use Martin Luther's teaching against certain Catholic Church regulations as a reason to overthrow all hold the status quo had on them.

This phenomenon terrified Martin Luther, who quickly sought to distance himself from it. Shortly after the disturbance erupted, Luther published a tract in which he openly called for the destruction of those involved, referring to the radicals as nothing more than "robbing and murdering hordes of peasants." It must be remembered that, although Luther was in rebellion against some elements of the mainstream, such as the Roman Catholic Church (and perhaps the Holy Roman Emperor), he was largely backed by the German nobility. His number one ally, after all, was the Elector of Saxony.

Martin Luther, therefore, wasted no time in siding with the upper classes in this case and made it known that he wished for the disturbance to immediately cease. Luther's wishes would be fulfilled when the uprising was squashed and Thomas Müntzer himself was hauled into custody and executed. Müntzer had attempted to spark a larger rebellion in the region of Thuringia, but many of the peasantry abandoned the cause when the regional powers rallied against them.

Of those who decided to remain, some 6,000 were killed and another 600 taken captive. Among those taken prisoner were Thomas Müntzer and Heinrich Pfeifer; both were tortured and forced to recant. Their heads were then chopped off and impaled on pikes.

Luther had begun his protestations against the Catholic Church in opposition to heavy-handedness, yet when it came to those who were too radical for his taste, he viewed their annihilation as quite justifiable. As expressed in his "Against the Robbing and Murdering Hordes of Peasants," he maintained, "It is just as when one must kill a mad dog; if you do not strike him, he will strike you, and a whole land with you." Ironically, Catholic authorities, as well as Protestant ones, began to use Martin Luther's own words as a justification to squash Reformation-inspired peasant rebellions of all kinds. It is indeed ironic that Luther, a man who kicked off a desire to pull away from authoritarian religious doctrine, began to openly denounce those he disagreed with—or even those who just happened to disagree with him!

This was indicated when, shortly after his publication of *Against the Murderous, Thieving Hordes of Peasants*, he wrote an open letter to the previous text in which he ominously proclaimed, "I must warn those who criticize my book to hold their tongues and to be careful not to make a mistake and lose their own heads." Luther was obviously ready to not only verbally combat his opponents but render physical force if need be.

In Switzerland, meanwhile, Huldrych Zwingli was making some major waves. In 1522, he had weighed in on a controversy regarding fasting during Lent. Several parishioners had decided to break the rule to abstain from meat, and Zwingli supported their decision. He even published a tract about it called "The Freedom of Choice in the Selection of Food."

In this work, Huldrych Zwingli insisted that "fasting was a human tradition, not a divine injunction, and therefore was a question for the conscience of the individual Christian, not a matter which the authorities should legislate." Zwingli also was quite adept at using

Scripture to justify his arguments—so much so that local officials decided to reform the rules pertaining to Lent if the religious orthodoxy could not find equally compelling scriptural arguments to back up their traditions.

After artfully laying out why dietary habits should not be controlled by the Catholic Church, Zwingli and his followers then moved on to tackle the argument over the veneration of saints. Zwingli opposed it. Zwingli also challenged the Catholic practice of enforcing celibacy among the priesthood. Zwingli insisted that since early church leaders such as the Apostle Peter had been married, there was no reason to issue a blanket ban on marriage upon the clergy. The argument was a personal one for Huldrych Zwingli since he was part of a clandestine marriage of his own—wed to a widow by the name of Anna Reinhart.

It's important to note that Martin Luther also took a wife around this time. His marriage stemmed from a rather dramatic episode in 1523 when he aided the escape of a nun named Katharina von Bora from a convent. As it turns out, Katharina was not in the convent by choice but was placed there by her father shortly after her mother had passed away. Her father eventually remarried, and Katharina was left in the convent simply for the convenience of her father. Hearing of the plight of this unhappy nun, Luther helped Katharina and eleven other nuns leave the convent that was holding them by smuggling the sisters out of the place in herring barrels.

After securing her release, Martin Luther placed Katharina in the care of a prominent lawyer named Philip Reichenbach. Katherina was in her mid-twenties at the time, and back in the 1500s, the options for a young woman like Katherina were rather limited. Since most women were not allowed to be their own breadwinners, typically the best route for security was through marriage. Luther found himself in the role of matchmaker, trying to introduce Katharina to potential suitors who could give her a home.

The suitors Luther provided all fell through, however. In the meantime, Luther, who was in his forties at the time, found himself falling in love with Katherina. This growing fondness culminated in their marriage on June 13, 1525. Other Protestants followed the example of both Martin Luther and Huldrych Zwingli as it pertained to celibacy and the right of Christians to marry.

At any rate, the common theme of all the arguments Zwingli raised was that the Bible should be the ultimate authority of Christian life and not the Roman Catholic Church or local governing officials. This view, which was indeed on par with Martin Luther's and was clearly explained in Huldrych Zwingli's *The Clarity and Certainty of the Word of God*. In a similar fashion to Martin Luther, he also delivered up theses. Yes, just like Luther had dished out his Ninety-five Theses, Zwingli crafted his own *Sixty-Seven Articles*, in which he went to great lengths to explain where he felt the Church needed serious reform.

It was in 1525 that Zwingli and his followers achieved a major success when the local city council of Zurich decided to formally abolish the requirement of mass—allowing citizens to carry out communion services in their own fashion and, more importantly, in their own language. Rather than Latin, which most Swiss didn't understand, services could now be held in German. Huldrych Zwingli had achieved meaningful reform through peaceful means, even as Müntzer's peasant revolt was going down in flames.

But Zwingli's efforts would not remain bloodless ones. The first major sign of discord in Zwingli's Reformation was when a group of fellow Swiss reformers decided that they didn't want to follow the Catholic tradition of baptizing infants. They argued that the New Testament Christians never had infants baptized, only adults. Therefore, they determined that only adults should be baptized in their day, as well. Like Martin Luther before him, Huldrych Zwingli apparently considered this too extreme of a position to take.

Zwingli wished to keep the baptism practice the Catholic Church already had in place and derided the baptismal reformers as "anti-baptists," or as they would later be known, "Anabaptists." To Zwingli's great dismay, however, Anabaptist ideology began to catch on in the Swiss city of Zurich, leading some parents to refuse to have their babies baptized. As lay preachers rose to baptize or re-baptize adult Christians, Zwingli questioned the motives of the instigators.

Rather than feeling their efforts were divinely inspired, Zwingli came to believe that these were just attention-getters who had a measureless thirst for fame. Things then took a rather ugly turn in 1526 when the local government attempted to thwart the movement by declaring that anyone who persisted in defying official Church doctrine on baptism would be put to death by drowning. This is said to have been "a form of punishment deliberately chosen to mock Anabaptist practice."

Although Zwingli had denounced the more radical Swiss reformers, soon after a major crackdown on the Anabaptists he, too, was called into question. He was asked to meet with none other than Johann Eck, who had questioned Luther at the Diet of Worms, to speak at a similar disputation in the Swiss city of Baden. Unlike Luther, who had met the challenge delivered to him by Eck, Zwingli refused, and this refusal alone was enough to have him labeled a heretic.

This meant that all of Zwingli's previously written works were now considered heretical, as well. Although Zwingli was not exactly a militant before, after he was condemned a heretic, he would certainly become one. Unlike the Anabaptists, who tended to suffer as persecuted pacifists, he was ready to lead an aggressive faction of Swiss reformers.

Martin Luther, for his part, was by now just as much against Zwingli as the Catholics were. In his 1528 piece entitled *Confession Concerning Christ's Supper*, he quite unabashedly declared, "I regard Zwingli as an un-Christian, with all his teaching, for he holds and teaches no part of the Christian faith rightly. He is seven times worse than when he was a papist." These were pretty harsh words from a man who had been so severely persecuted for his own beliefs.

Zwingli ultimately met his end on October 11, 1531, when a Catholic army was raised against him and his reformers in Zurich. Huldrych Zwingli himself is said to have died on the battlefield with a sword in hand—very much living up to Jesus' cautioning admonition that "those who live by the sword" would also surely "die by the sword." It is said that the Catholic troops who came across Zwingli's mortally-wounded form attempted to show mercy by offering Zwingli the chance to partake in the last rites of a Catholic believer. Zwingli had not become a reformer to turn back at the last minute, however. Instead, Huldrych Zwingli refused and was delivered a mortal blow by one of the troop's swords. As a final insult, it is said that they then burned his body and had his ashes sprinkled over the excrement of pigs. It was indeed a terrible end for this would-be reformer. At the height of his reformation efforts, Zwingli had envisioned an entire Christian confederation, in which a reformed church could be established, being created in Switzerland. His death, however, managed to crush his burgeoning movement in Zurich. With Huldrych Zwingli's death, Martin Luther remained the best-known middle-of-the-road reformer.

Chapter 6 – From Melchiorite to Mennonite—Some Additional Strains of Reformation

"Scholars have argued that without humanism the Reformation could not have succeeded, and it is certainly difficult to imagine the Reformation occurring without the knowledge of languages, the critical handling of sources, the satirical attacks on clerics and scholastics, and the new national feeling that a generation of humanists provided. On the other hand, the long-term success of the humanist owed something to the Reformation. In Protestant schools and universities classical culture found a permanent home."

- Steven Ozment

As Martin Luther stayed the course in Wittenberg, more radical sects continued to sprout up all around him. In 1533, the Netherlands saw a brief but incredibly dramatic movement emerge under the leadership of a German furrier by the name of Melchior Hoffman. Known as Melchiorism, this reform movement preached an apocalyptic vision of the "imminent return" of Christ.

At one point, Hoffman even came to believe a fellow prophetic visionary who informed him that Christ would return once Melchior was arrested and thrown in prison. It's hard to fathom how his arrest would trigger the Second Coming, but Melchior seemed to be an enthusiastic supporter of the notion, and as such, he went out of his way to fulfill the prophecy by getting arrested before the year was out.

The original prophecy claimed that Christ would return after Melchior was imprisoned for six months. But, as far as anyone can tell, Christ didn't return in 1533, and rather than being released after six months, Melchior died in prison several years later. After Melchior was out of the picture, the next leader of the so-called Melchiorites was a man named Jan Mathijs. Under the leadership of Jan Mathijs, the Melchiorites set up a base in the region of Westphalia (northwestern Germany), in the town of Münster.

Anabaptists also increasingly flocked to the city and began to call it their "New Jerusalem." It wasn't long before tensions among Luther's followers, the Melchiorites, Anabaptists, Catholics, and others became incredibly strained. Followers of Martin Luther—Lutherans—were suspected of being in league with Catholic authorities, and the Anabaptists and Melchiorites began to fear that the Lutherans would send in the Catholic troops to annihilate them.

Things came to a head when the Anabaptists, under the leadership of one Hermann Redeker, converged on city hall en masse, brandishing swords. The local Catholic bishop sent a small militia to engage the reformers, and the show of force convinced them to sue for peace. As soon as the truce was declared, however, the Melchiorite Jan Mathijs moved in and reestablished his own power base. Mathijis is said to have become so influential in the city at one point that he convinced city authorities to persecute and imprison his rivals.

However, Jan's reign came to an end when, after having a dream in which he was victorious against the Catholic army, he charged off to face Catholic troops—who easily dispatched with the zealous reformer.

It was after the death of Jan Mathijs that another Melchiorite, a man named Jan van Leiden, took over the Münster movement. Jan van Leiden had tremendous sway over Münster's city council, so much so that he was eventually able to get the city council dismissed outright.

Then, in the fall of 1534, van Leiden unabashedly declared Münster to be a theocracy under his guidance. This radical reformer declared that he had been given power over emperors, kings, princes, and all the power of the Earth. In his power trip, Jan van Leiden sought to liken himself to King David or King Solomon, ruling over a religious city-state. His most faithful followers sought to confirm this claim of authority by issuing a prediction that their so-called King Jan would eventually take over the Earth in its entirety, and eliminate his rivals.

It's hard to believe that Luther's initial calls for reformation could lead to such radical developments, and Luther himself was perhaps more dumbfounded by this development than anyone else. Luther had hoped to create a united Protestant front but ended up facing the reality that his break with the Catholic Church had led to several others rising to thrust forth their own unique interpretations of Scripture—which were just as often contrary to as inspired by his own teachings.

Martin Luther must have realized that the great strength of the Catholic Church was its dogged quest for uniformity since he now had to endure the rise of a seemingly endless variety of factions and denominations coming to fruition. The most Luther could settle for was his own Protestant brand, which had become known as Lutheranism, to carry the torch of his teachings. Most galling, however, was the fact that Luther, who was initially persecuted by the Catholic Church for deviating from official Church doctrine, found himself having to encourage persecution of rival sects that he had found to be dangerously heretical.

He encouraged the squashing of the peasant rebellion, the Anabaptists, and many others who ideologically rubbed him the wrong way. By being an authoritarian controller of what he viewed to be correct doctrine, was Luther becoming the very thing he hated when he rebelled against the Roman Catholics in the first place? Yet for Luther, heavy-handed crackdowns were preferable to having to deal with some of the more radical results of the Reformation.

The previously mentioned King Jan, for example, had begun running the city of Münster as a dictator. Other Protestants viewed one of King Jan's most egregious actions to be the use of Old Testament Scripture to justify polygamous marriages. Thanks to the support of Jan van Leiden, these polygamous unions were among the first the Christian world had seen. King Jan not only allowed polygamous marriage but belligerently enforced the practice when church members objected.

One woman, for example, objected to her husband having more than one wife and was consequently executed. King Jan was even known to have executed a spouse or two of his own on similar grounds. According to Reformation scholar and writer Andrew Atherstone, when it was all said and done, the poor "citizens of Münster lived in abject fear under this Melchiorite reign of terror."

With such absolute anarchy erupting in certain Reformation circles, Luther saw no clear alternative to this chaos except to vigorously fight back against views he considered heretical. As for King Jan, his so-called tyrannical reign came to an end on June 25, 1535, when Catholic troops were brought forward to crush yet another Protestant insurgency. In the aftermath, it is said that Münster's streets were strewn with corpses and awash with blood.

As for King Jan? He, like so many other radical reformers, paid the ultimate price—he was taken out to the "Münster market." This was the sort of place one could find a butcher in a stall slicing up fresh slabs of meat for eager customers. But it wasn't animal flesh that was butchered at the market on that day—it was King Jan. He was brutally tortured by having his flesh ripped apart with red-hot iron tongs.

The pain must have been unbearable, and King Jan was only relieved of it when his throat was slit and a knife was shoved into his heart. After being killed in this manner, he and the bodies of two of his compatriots were placed in iron cages and hung from the steeple of Münster's now-infamous landmark—St. Lambert's Church. Although the mortal remains of Jan and company are long gone, the iron cages remain suspended as an ominous warning to this very day.

After this latest militant strain of Anabaptists was put to rest, a newly-christened pacifist group that would become known as the Mennonites would take root. The Mennonites were founded by a former Catholic priest named Menno Simmons. Menno joined the Melchiorites in 1536, and he rose to leadership of the movement in 1540. Soon thereafter, his followers ceased to be known as Melchiorites and instead were referred to as Mennonites.

Menno made his way through much of northern Germany and the Netherlands, preaching his doctrine on baptism and the power of faith. But the big difference between the Mennonites and the Melchiorites was the fact that the Mennonites were taught to spread their message through pacifistic means. Rather than taking over city councils and trying to govern communities, the Mennonites (much like the early Christians) simply sought to change the hearts and minds of those who heard them—persuading them through preaching rather than force.

Even though other Protestants and Catholics still disagreed with much of the Mennonite teaching, you would think they would at least appreciate the non-violent nature of the Mennonite movement. Yet, Holy Roman Emperor Charles V made it his personal mission to stamp the Mennonites out and even offered a reward should someone bring Mennonite leader Menno into his custody.

Needless to say, the Mennonites did not have the powerful political backers that Martin Luther did. Martin Luther was a true power broker in his day and, in many ways, was viewed as a kind of "Protestant pope" in the way that he could effectively maneuver through all the intrigue between the Catholic Church and rival Protestant groups. And Luther's views of the Mennonites were not too encouraging. He viewed them as schismatic heretics who consigned children to hell since they refused to engage in infant baptism.

With both Catholics and Lutherans against them, the Mennonites were persecuted so badly that, for most of them, the only real option was to flee. The Mennonite diaspora would have these Protestant reformers traveling far and wide. A new base was found for some time in the Netherlands, and eventually, many more would migrate all the way across the Atlantic Ocean to America, where Mennonite communities can still be found. From Melchiorite to Mennonite, this tradition sprung from the Reformation remains strong.

Chapter 7 – England's Reformation Begins

"Alas, how can the poor souls live in concord when you preachers sow amongst them in your sermons debate and discord? They look to you for light and darkness. Amend these crimes, I exhort you, and set forth God's word truly, both by true preaching and giving a good example, or else I, whom God has appointed his vicar and high minister here, will see these divisions extinct, and these enormities corrected."

    -    King Henry VIII

As the Reformation unfolded on the European continent, across the English Channel, a British king called Henry VIII was paying very close attention to the developments. As Henry saw the propagation of Protestant faith across Europe, he initially saw it as his chance to present himself as a stalwart defender of Catholicism against the newfound heretics. And he wasted no time in doing it.

Just a short time after Martin Luther's infamous showdown at the Diet of Worms in 1521, in fact, King Henry VIII put together a carefully worded "doctrinal treatise" in which he took Martin Luther's beliefs to task. A hallmark of Lutheran belief stemmed from Luther's work—*The Babylonian Captivity of the Church*—in which the reformer maintained that the only two sacraments that mattered were the Lord's Supper and baptism.

Henry was a fierce opponent of this assertion, standing by the Catholic Church's seven standard sacraments. King Henry VIII wrote a polemical text called *Assertio Septem Sacramentorum* (*Defense of the Seven Sacraments*), in which he made his beliefs on this matter crystal clear. He also made his distaste of Luther obvious when he declared that he was nothing more than "a knavish little friar."

Among other things, Henry also described Luther as being one who "spews out viper's venom" and was leading the whole flock astray. All of this, of course, was music to the Roman Catholic pope's ears. Luther may have secured his physical protection through the Elector of Saxony, but he was not out of the reach of King Henry VIII's full-on bombastic verbal assault. The pope was so happy, in fact, that he officially bestowed upon King Henry the title of "Fidei Defensor," or "Defender of the Faith."

The official faith of England at this time, of course, was the Roman Catholic religion. Yes, even though King Henry eventually kicked off his own reformation in England, in the early days of the Protestant Reformation, he was indeed a defender of the Catholic faith. But even though Henry cast himself as the defensive wall against the epidemic of European Protestantism, some strains of the movement did indeed seep through to the British Isles.

Martin Luther's works were being translated into various languages at a rapid clip, and some of them found their way to English shores. One of the places where these migratory theological works surfaced was none other than Cambridge. Here it is said that the works were well received by the colleagues of a certain Thomas Bilney. Bilney had gone through his own period of reform when he read a recently translated copy of the New Testament in which the words of Saint Paul, which declared "that Christ Jesus came into the world to save sinners, of whom I am the worst," struck him to the core.

Bilney was moved by the concept that even one of the Bible's greatest saints considered himself one of the worst. If even Paul could do nothing to save himself, it only seemed to clarify the Protestant teaching that works are meaningless and it is only through faith that one can be saved. Bilney began to openly speak of what he had learned with others at Cambridge, and soon many of his associates were also moved to reconsider Catholic teachings.

During this same time, a British scholar named William Tyndale began to work on developing a new translation of the Bible that did not depend on the Catholic Church's Latin translation but rather the original Hebrew and Greek languages it was written in. It was a major undertaking—one you might think his countrymen would have been proud of—but according to an English law called the Constitutions of Oxford, written back in 1408, it was considered illegal for such a translation to be made.

It may seem a bit bizarre that it would be illegal to merely develop a new translation of the Bible, but this was indeed the case. Knowing that his work could get him in some real hot water in England, Tyndale hightailed out of Britain and made his way to Luther's backyard—arriving first in Cologne, and then the city of Worms. It was while in Worms that Tyndale managed to finish his translation of the New Testament in its entirety in 1526.

With his new translation in hand, Tyndale took full advantage of the printing press and began to print out several copies, which made their way to Britain. It's amazing to think that a Bible printed in one's own language would be so controversial, but for the Catholic Church, it was a very serious matter. As soon as Catholics in Britain got wind of what was happening, they did everything they could to seize the new translations making their way to Britain and have them burned.

Yes, it's absurd to think of Catholic priests burning Bibles, but that is indeed what happened. Tyndale was also thoroughly condemned by the Catholic scholar, Bishop Tunstall, who supposedly studied Tyndale's translated text and declared that there were some 2,000 errors in his translation. Citing these supposed errors, Bishop Tunstall demanded that all copies of the Tyndale translations be found and destroyed lest they lead the faithful astray.

Tyndale's Bible translation was indeed at odds with the traditional Latin translation of the Catholic Church. The Greek word *metanoeo*, which the Latin version understood as "penance," was translated into English as "repent." This slight change was very significant since it seemed to undermine the Catholic belief in having to do penance—an integral part of the Catholic faith. Incensed by these "dangerous translations," prominent statesmen and cardinal Thomas Wolsey led the charge of a massive search for biblical books and people associated with their circulation.

Books burned, and several went to prison in this effort to stamp out the newly-translated texts. Among those taken into custody over these heretical translations was a British scholar named John Frith. Frith was only let go after promising to stay within ten miles of Oxford. But Frith wasn't going to follow these orders and instead left Britain altogether, settling in Antwerp where Tyndale had taken up residence.

It was during this exile that Frith wrote the important reformatory text, the *Disputation of Purgatory divided into Three Books*, in which he presented his opinion that purgatory was an erroneous Catholic teaching. Tyndale also hammered away at Catholic doctrine with his own Protestant texts, largely patterned after Luther's original argument that Christians are saved by faith rather than works. Tyndale made the most waves when he wrote his seminal work, *The Obedience of a Christian Man*.

In this work, Tyndale made it clear that he believed man's ultimate allegiance should not be to a king or any government, but to God alone. The establishment did not like this at all since they believed Tyndale's liberating doctrine would spread dissent and rebellion among the masses. However, Tyndale deflected criticism by pointing out that, although he argued that man's ultimate allegiance was to God, the Bible was clear in its directive to submit to local governance.

Meanwhile, Tyndale absolutely excoriated Catholic priests for what he perceived to be their preoccupation with rituals and tradition. He sarcastically referenced their reverence for "holy water, holy fire, holy bread, holy salt, hallowed bells, holy wax, holy boughs, holy candles, and holy ashes" while presenting an apparent disregard for the Bible. His critics, on the other hand, maintained that the average person would not be able to understand Scripture unless it was filtered through the official interpretation sanctioned by the Catholic Church.

Tyndale wasn't buying it, however, and felt the Catholic Church was verging on a conspiratorial cover-up in its refusal to allow the English people to read Bibles translated into their own language. Tyndale claimed that Rome was purposefully keeping the British faithful in the dark and stated, "To keep us from knowledge of the truth, they do all things in Latin. They pray in Latin, they christen in Latin, they bless in Latin, they give absolution in Latin: only curse they in the English tongue."

In his attacks on the clergy, Tyndale also made an appeal directly to the king of England to weigh in on the controversy. Using a similar strategy as the German reformers, Tyndale sought to stir up national sentiment in the kingdom against the intervention of Rome. But King Henry VIII, a strong critic of Luther who had just been honored by the pope as the "Defender of the Faith," had yet to be swayed.

Mirroring Tyndale's efforts of persuasion, another British reformer in exile named Simon Fish wrote a piece called *A Supplication for the Beggars*, which he presented as an actual complaint from the blind, the sick, and the lame lodged against the invasion of England by a multitude of ecclesiastics who had come down on Britain like "ravenous wolves." Fish's bombastic tract urged that these interlopers be driven out and "whipped naked through every market town."

But King Henry was indeed on the side of Catholic hardliners at this point, and rather than drive out the Catholic clergy, he allowed his minions to do their best to drive out the Protestant reformers. Now, books were not the only thing burned, but in many cases, individuals went up in flames, as well. When caught, reformers were threatened with being burned at the stake, and under the terrible duress of torture, some were forced to recant.

One of the most famous to retract his Protestant beliefs under this pressure was Thomas Bilney, who caved and offered a full recantation in 1527 when confronted by Wolsey. His life was spared, but he would live to regret it. Unable to simply go back to his old way of life, Bilney broke down in 1531 and began to preach his views in the countryside of Norwich. Here he came upon a former nun converted to Protestantism and handed her a translated text of Tyndale's New Testament.

This bold act alerted the authorities and led to Bilney being burned at the stake shortly thereafter. The execution of Bilney seemed to kick off a spate of hardline crackdowns that lasted from late 1531 on into 1532. The persecution was so intense that, at one point, even people who were already dead were being burned at the stake. This was the case with William Tracy, who made his allegiance clear on his deathbed by refusing Catholic tradition and proclaiming "I accept none in heaven or in earth to be mediator between me and God, but only Jesus Christ."

This meant that Tracy denied the Catholic Church the chance to perform his last rites and died (albeit of natural causes) a heretic in the eyes of the Church. Since he was already dead, the Church had to settle for desecrating his corpse to set an example. So, his body was dug up and posthumously burned in effigy. It was during this purge of Protestants that John Frith was finally captured in 1531. Frith was immediately sent to London's Tower—that medieval dungeon of a holding cell—to await the kangaroo court the Catholics called a trial.

While Frith was locked up, Tyndale wrote him words of encouragement, extolling the prisoner, "Your cause is Christ's gospel, a light that must be fed with [the] blood of faith. Rejoice and be glad, for great is your reward in heaven." Frith stood trial shortly thereafter, and his chief prosecutor was a certain Bishop John Stokesley, who charged that Frith was nothing more than a "child of wickedness and darkness" and that he had committed the most detestable heresies. Stokesley also argued that Frith should receive the ultimate punishment, lest he "infect the Lord's flock with [his] heresy."

Until this point, the king of England, the man who had been hailed as the "Defender of the Faith" by the Catholic Church, had supported the hardline stance against the Reformation. But mitigating factors in the king's own life—or at least his marriage bed—would soon make the king change his stance dramatically. The king, who was at this point married to the Spanish princess, Katherine of Aragon, was desperate to have a male heir to the throne.

But, as of yet, his wife had only produced a daughter—Princess Mary. As the years went by and Katherine's miscarriages added up, King Henry became convinced that his wife would not be able to provide him with a male heir. Henry wanted to continue the Tudor line of which he was a part, and without a son he would not be able to do so. This put him in a terrible bind. He began to feel that his marriage was cursed. This is no exaggeration, since he took the words of Scripture in Leviticus (20:21) to heart. This verse of Scripture advised that, if a man were to marry his brother's wife, "it is an impurity."

King Henry had indeed married his brother's wife—at least, his former wife—since she was the widow of his brother, Prince Arthur. Henry began to openly wonder if this perceived violation of Leviticus could be the reason behind his troubles in securing a male heir. Since the Catholic Church generally forbade divorce, the king sought out ways in which the marriage might become annulled. The pope, however, refused to fulfill the king's wishes. This left the king scrambling to figure out an alternative. After consulting with Cardinal Wolsey and the pope's legate, Cardinal Campeggio, he was advised to have Katherine give up her marriage and join a convent so that Henry would be free to enter a new marriage.

As one might imagine, Katherine was not quite so thrilled with the prospect of stepping down as queen to become a nun. She was appalled at what was being suggested of her and sent a direct appeal to the pope. The king, in the meantime, was infuriated that his advisers were unable to find a better solution for him and had Cardinal Wolsey dismissed. He ended up with a new adviser who had been a previous associate of Wolsey, Thomas Cromwell.

It was Cromwell who began to conspire with the king about the possibility of using his own power to get what he wanted. The argument presented to Henry was twofold. It was determined that King Henry did indeed have solid reasoning to get an annulment due to the biblical grounds mentioned in Leviticus. Secondly, it was argued that papal authority could not command the king. King Henry always knew that he could try to force the issue, but, cherishing his role as "Defender of the Faith," he was hesitant to anger the pope.

Nevertheless, as he continued to consider increasing his powers and diminishing Rome's, Henry began to throw his weight around when it came to theological matters in England. In the spring of 1532, for example, he issued his "Supplication Against the Ordinaries," which argued that rather than the clergy deciding who would be charged with heresy, any such grievances needed to be directly addressed to King Henry.

Coming on the heels of the great persecution that had been launched in late 1531, this petition signaled a tremendous turnaround in England's handling of the Protestant Reformation. King Henry wasn't agreeing with the Protestants, but he was at least making the case that any grievances leveled against them should be brought to him before Roman Catholic clergy started lighting matches and burning folks at the stake.

Catholic clergy did not like this, however, and refused to recognize the decree. The following May, this led King Henry to declare, "We thought that the clergy of our realm had been our subjects wholly, but now we have well perceived that they be but half our subjects, yea, and scarce our subject: for all the prelates at their consecration make an oath to the pope, clear contrary to the oath that they make us, so they seem to be his subjects, and not ours."

These dire words were enough to get the clergy in line, and shortly thereafter, they formally conceded to royal decree, pledging that their actions would henceforth need to be justified by the king. In 1533, shortly after this recognition, King Henry finally made the move to put away his wife and remarry in complete defiance of the pope. His new Queen—Anne Boleyn—was decried as nothing more than a harlot in Catholic circles, but besides disparaging the union from afar, there was nothing the Roman Catholic clergy could do.

The king's power was then further cemented into British law in the fall of 1534 with the creation of the Act of Supremacy, which clearly stated that King Henry was to be considered the "only Supreme Head in Earth of the Church of England." According to this act, the king now had serious reformative power when it came to "all errors, heresies, and other enormities and abuses." Even though King Henry was previously against the Reformation, this act unilaterally made England a part of it since Henry managed to scale back any real power or control the pope had over English religious affairs.

Ironically enough, the king's break with Catholic authority led to a persecution of the very Catholic faithful of whom Henry had previously been dubbed the defender. For when Catholic diehards began to speak out against the king's actions, they—like the Protestants before them—ended up losing their lives. One of the most sensational of these persecutions of zealous Catholics occurred in April of 1534 when the so-called Holy Maid—a Catholic nun named Elizabeth Barton—was hung and decapitated for speaking out against the king.

In the early 1530s, Barton had made several prophesies about King Henry that were deemed seditious. She subsequently developed a brief following among English Catholics before being rounded up, tried for treason, and put to death for her beliefs. Many more executions followed in 1535, including some high-profile figures such as Cardinal John Fisher and Sir Thomas More—who were previously key players in the persecution and suppression of the Protestants.

Further internal reform of the Church of England took place in 1536, with new measures such as the insistence that the Ten Commandments be translated into English. It is rather stunning to think that men like Firth were killed over English translations of the Bible just a few years prior, only to have the king himself suddenly sanction the English translation of the Ten Commandments. The new regulations also criticized traditional Catholic practices such as "pilgrimages to local shrines [and] the offering of money or votive candles before religious relics," among other things.

But there was more to come. Going completely full circle in 1538, the king, who had previously turned a blind eye to the persecution of translators of the Bible, decreed that a full English translation should be openly distributed to church members. This led to the publication of the so-called Great Bible translation that was rendered by Miles Coverdale in April of 1539. This was the first authorized edition of the Bible—sanctioned by King Henry VIII himself.

The preface to the Great Bible, written by Archbishop Cranmer, urged the English to cherish the Scripture, stating that they were "a better jewel in our house than either gold or silver." This urging of the average Briton to have a Bible of their own was indeed a stark contrast to the previous years of hunting down anyone who so dared to read the Bible for themselves. It seemed that the king had put his finger on the scale for the Protestants after all, but it was a little more complicated than that.

While the king sought to present himself as the main authority for church doctrine rather than the pope, the old "Defender of the Faith" himself was still a stickler for many standard Catholic doctrines. The king had his own problems in the meantime. He had become increasingly paranoid as his inner circle conspired around him, so when Cromwell–seeking to rid himself of Queen Anne's influence–made up stories about her being unfaithful, the king took the bait.

Henry ended up having his own wife executed in 1536. It is incredibly cynical to consider it, but many have wondered if the king took this route as an expedient means of ridding himself of yet another wife who could not produce a son for him. Queen Anne had not yet been able to bear a son when she was beheaded. At any rate, upon her death, Henry wasted little time in taking a new wife–Jane Seymour.

It was Queen Jane who would finally give birth to the son that King Henry VIII so desperately craved. She gave birth to Prince Edward but, shortly thereafter, perished of septicemia, leaving the proud new father once again a widower. King Henry the VIII's next marriage would not be to bring about a son but was, instead, a marriage of political convenience.

Ever since England went rogue, there was a risk of Catholic powers such as France or the Holy Roman Empire deciding to intervene militarily. Although King Henry VIII had been initially against Martin Luther and all the other German reformers, he now saw them as potential allies. So, when the opportunity arose to marry a German noblewoman–Anne of Cleves–he agreed to do so out of sheer political pragmatism. However, the king was not too thrilled with his new wife and, at one point, even called her downright repulsive.

The marriage was annulled after just six months, in 1540. Shortly thereafter, the king tried his luck at marriage again by marrying Catherine Howard, the Duke of Norfolk's niece. This marriage wouldn't last very long, either. This queen proved to be rather scandalous and was caught having an affair with a man by the name of

Thomas Culpeper. Both Catherine and Culpeper were executed for this offense, with Queen Catherine—the latest wife of King Henry to be beheaded—sent to the chopping block the day before St. Valentine's Day—February 13, 1542.

Shortly after the death of Catherine, King Henry seemed to have a change of heart regarding some of the religious liberty he had previously bestowed. In a complete reversal of his previously championing of Bible reading, he decided that not everyone should have access to Scripture. The king seemed to fear that too many people were getting the wrong ideas from Scripture and worried that it would lead to insurrection against him. As such, in 1543, he issued the Act for the Advancement of True Religion, which stipulated that there would be restrictions on who could read the Bible.

The act deemed that "women, servants, and laborers" should not be allowed to read Scripture on their own and furthermore dictated that they could be punished if found with their own translation of Scripture. Many English Protestants who were hopeful that the English king could lead them to a complete reformation of religion were greatly dismayed by the king's actions.

As the reformer John Hooper put it, "As far as true religion is concerned, idolatry is nowhere in greater vigor. Our king has destroyed the pope, but not popery. The impious mass, the most shameful celibacy of the clergy, the invocation of saints, auricular confession, superstitious abstinence from meats, and purgatory, were never before held by the people in greater esteem than at the present moment."

The king, meanwhile, had married for one final time in the summer of 1543 when he wed a widow by the name of Catherine Parr. Catherine herself was a supporter of the Reformation, and it is said that she continually tried to persuade her husband to be more supportive of the cause.

Henry was getting older, however, and seemed to be firmly stuck in his ways. Therefore, his strange hybrid form of anti-pope—yet still largely anti-Protestant doctrines—remained. And they would continue even some time after King Henry VIII's death in 1547. Martin Luther, the initial instigator of the Reformation, in the meantime, had died the prior year, in 1546. Both deaths would mark a sea change in the next phases of the larger Reformation.

Chapter 8 – The Rise of Calvinism

"When they inquire into predestination, let them remember that they are penetrating into the recesses of the divine wisdom, where he who rushes forward securely and confidently, instead of satisfying his curiosity will enter an inextricable labyrinth. For it is not right that man should with impunity pry into things that the Lord has been pleased to conceal within himself, and scan that sublime eternal wisdom that it is his pleasure that we should not apprehend but adore, that therein also his perfections may appear. Those secrets of his will, which he has seen it meet to manifest, are revealed in his word—revealed insofar as he knew to be conducive to our interest and welfare."

- John Calvin

Second perhaps only to Martin Luther himself, one of the greatest forces at work in the Reformation was John Calvin. John—or as he was known to the French, Jean Cauvin—began his efforts at reform in France. It was during the persecution of Protestants in 1535 that Calvin fled France for Switzerland. Calvin first set up shop in the town of Basel. Here, he wrote long tracts about his religious theories, one of which was entitled *The Institutes of the Christian Religion*.

The book was dedicated to the then king of France—King Francois I—and included a heartfelt request for the king to put an end to his heavy-handedness against the Protestants of France. Calvin insisted that the Protestants were being maligned by their opponents, and requested an inquest into what he viewed as little more than a slander campaign. Another major argument that Calvin made was that the efforts of reformers were by no means a new invention.

Calvin made the case that what the reformers were attempting to accomplish was completely consistent with apostolic and early church doctrine. Furthermore, he made it known his position that he believed those who opposed the gospel—or at least his personal version of it—were "tools of Satan." It's not likely that Calvin's words addressed to the king had much impact, but as it so happens, the persecutions did come to a halt shortly thereafter: in the summer of 1535, the Edict of Coucy granted a general amnesty to the remaining Protestant reformers in France.

But this amnesty didn't come without a catch. As it stood, any and all who were deemed to be fugitives who had left France could only return and receive a pardon if they "renounced their heretical views within six months." The likes of hardline reformers such as John Calvin were obviously not going to suddenly renounce their so called heretical views simply to go back home. All John did was take advantage of the six-month grace period to return to France and take care of some personal matters.

But before this six-month window was out, John left France for good in 1536 rather than recant. He was only twenty-seven at the time and would live the rest of his years as a reformer in exile. After leaving France for the last time, he made his way to Geneva, Switzerland. Swiss cities had been home to several reform movements in the past, and Geneva had just passed legislation in 1536 ensuring the citizenry would be free of the authority of the Roman Catholic Church.

John Calvin began his work in Geneva by means of public lectures in which he argued his views on the Bible. Due to religious infighting, John Calvin was eventually expelled from Geneva in 1538. From there, he ended up in Strassburg, where he was made the pastor of a group of French-speaking Protestants. He was given this role by a prominent Protestant named Martin Bucer, who supposedly convinced John Calvin to take the position by reminding him of what happened to Jonah when he shirked the calling of God.

Jonah, according to Scripture, was the biblical prophet who was swallowed by a whale. Martin Bucer became John Calvin's number one advisor in all his affairs and eventually even turned into a matchmaker of sorts when he introduced John Calvin to an eligible widow named Idelette de Bure. Idelette had been a part of the Anabaptist faith that was dominant in Swiss cities at the time. After settling down in Strassburg, John Calvin began to write long treatises on his Protestant beliefs. Among them was his "Reply to Cardinal Sadoleto."

Written in 1539, this letter was indeed a reply to a certain Cardinal Sadoleto, who had previously crafted an open letter to reformers in Geneva, attempting to convince them to return to the Catholic faith. Sadoleto's letter stood out from other attempts to bring reformers back in line in that the cardinal's efforts seemed to be sincere—in fact, almost apologetic in nature—and openly admitted that the Roman Catholic Church did indeed need to face up to certain excesses and abuses of power.

But even given these concessions, Sadoleto tried to convince all who would read his words that there was still a place for them in the Roman Catholic Church. It's interesting to note that even though Calvin had been essentially run out of Geneva, he was still called upon at his new residence in Strassburg to answer the cardinal's entreaty. In his reply, Calvin hammered out the need for the Church to reform and made the case that the Reformation was not just about the abuses and corruption of the Church, but an effort to reform the "very heart" of Catholicism.

In this reply to Cardinal Sadoleto, Calvin went further than Martin Luther had in his Ninety-five Theses. When Martin Luther nailed his theses on that church door, he was indeed mainly seeking the reform of abuses and corruption of the Catholic Church, such as the sale of indulgences. Calvin, however, made it clear that he wasn't looking for reform as much as he was seeking revolution. He also made it clear that he and his associates were not "theological innovators" as detractors had charged, but rather, they were attempting to stay closer to the original principles of the New Testament than the Catholic Church had. During this time, he also wrote his own personal commentary on the New Testament book of Romans, as well as an extensive article that covered the Lord's Supper.

Close on the heels of these works, in 1540 and 1541, John Calvin and Martin Bucer toured the cities of Hagenau, Worms, and Regensburg, where they attended a series of theological debates that took place between Protestants and Catholics. Calvin found himself deeply disturbed by what he perceived as a terrible compromise in doctrine, amid the Protestants of Geneva. These divisions made him grow even more fond of the solidarity he had grown accustomed to in Strassburg.

John Calvin partially blamed the division he witnessed in Geneva on his own expulsion from the city. He knew this to be true, but all the same, when city authorities requested Calvin to return to his stewardship over the Protestant faithful, he claimed that he "shuddered at the very idea." This was the city that had thrown him out—why would he want to go back? Despite his misgivings, however, he finally did return as asked on September 13, 1541.

Calvin immediately set to work reforming the reformers, issuing his *Ecclesiastical Ordinances* in November of 1541. This work outlined Calvin's vision for how the church should be structured in Geneva and would eventually become a standard blueprint for many other churches far and wide. Calvin's church structure consisted of four primary roles in the church: deacons, elders, doctors, and pastors.

Calvin instructed his flock that pastors should corner the market when it came to preaching, spiritual counsel, and administration of sacraments. Doctors, on the other hand, should focus on matters of theology and engage in debates, lectures, or other similar speaking engagements. As for elders, Luther specifically instructed that there should be twelve elders selected from the laity. Deacons, meanwhile, were to focus on charity, such as aiding the impoverished and ill at health.

Beyond these directives for specific church roles, John Calvin's ordinances also reiterated his personal views on doctrinal issues such as baptism, the Lord's Supper, marriage, burial, visitation of the sick and prisoners, and the catechesis of children. As part of this new organization of the Protestants in Geneva, Calvin also established a council to oversee the whole of the operation. The council consisted of elders, pastors, and other church officials who routinely met and discussed the state of church affairs.

Often enough, this sort of religious oversight committee turned into nothing short of a tribunal when those accused of various sins they did not acknowledge or repent of were brought before the council for questioning. These sins ranged from adultery and blasphemy to simply accusations of being disrespectful in church. If those questioned refused to recant from their transgressions, they were suspended from the Lord's Supper, which essentially amounted to the Calvinist version of excommunication from the church.

To be clear, these were some fairly drastic reforms for many of Geneva's citizens, and not all supported them. One of Calvin's most prominent critics was a Swiss politician named Ami Perrin. Perrin objected to the scrutiny being placed upon everyone's personal lives and created a group of dissidents who went by the moniker of the "Children of Geneva." Due to their more liberal outlook, these objectors were later called the "Libertines."

Things came to a head when Ami Perrin's own spouse—Francoise—was brought before the council on charges of dancing. She was deemed guilty and thrown behind bars for the transgression. The situation was inflamed even further when the imprisoned woman's father was arrested for making remarks about Calvin being akin to "a Catholic priest at auricular confession who wanted to hear the details of everyone's sin."

John Calvin addressed some of the criticism being leveled at him in his 1550 work entitled *On the Scandals that Today Prevent Many People from Coming to the Pure Doctrine of the Gospel and Ruin Others*. Here Calvin was on both the defensive and offensive, as he defended his stance while simultaneously assaulting the character of those who dared disagree by calling them all a bunch of debauched fornicators who would rather follow the teachings of the pope than his recommended doctrine.

The strict oversight of Calvin's teaching was not the only thing that some objected to. For the more theologically minded, the most galling thing about Calvin wasn't that he didn't want people to dance—but rather that he believed everyone's ultimate destiny had already been determined. Known as predestination, this central tenant of Calvinism is the notion that God has determined ahead of time who goes to Heaven and who goes to hell. Today in Christian circles, the concept is usually mentioned with the more mundane vernacular of "once saved, always saved."

Even though Calvin had ignited a major debate over whether salvation is preordained by an all-knowing, omniscient God, the truth is, this debate has raged amongst Christians from the very beginning of Christianity. From the earliest of times, some Christians had believed that once you professed faith in Christ, absolutely nothing could take you out of his hand. Others, however, were certain that salvation was not absolute, and if one fell far enough astray, one could lose their salvation.

But there were (and are) severe problems with both these concepts. If a Christian believes in the "once saved, always saved" doctrine, it presents the danger of giving people a "license to sin." If believers' salvation is guaranteed no matter what, they could do all manner of heinous things between the first time they get saved and their death and still get to Heaven just fine.

On the other hand, if a Christian adopts a doctrine of salvation that is not absolute or somehow limited in scope, this understanding brings unforeseen consequences, as well. For example, if Christians could sin and suddenly lose their salvation, this would put them on some rather shaky ground, and no one's salvation would be guaranteed. Catholics themselves had long struggled with the idea that they could lose their salvation, and, generally, it resulted in many Catholics obsessively compulsively counting rosary beads, making the sign of the cross, and begging God for forgiveness every single time a perceived transgression occurred "lest their name be blotted out from the Book of Life."

But even if someone obsessively prays for forgiveness over every perceived offense, what if they don't have the chance to repent before dying? Furthermore, what if they committed sins that they didn't even realize were sins, such as sins of the heart? Jesus, after all, taught that to look at one's brother with hate was the same as outright killing him. Think of someone in a road rage incident screaming at a fellow motorist in full-on anger and then dying from a heart attack shortly thereafter—no chance for a sinner's prayer there. Did they lose their salvation?

Many Christians today would have a problem with the idea that the God they believe in would cast them to the side so easily. Yet, if God could look past one sin, then what about the others? Are some sins forgivable and others are not? Then again, if all sins are automatically forgiven through the finished work of the cross (as some Christians contend), what would be the point of repeatedly requesting forgiveness for something already forgiven? And, for some, this logic would seem to license all manner of unchecked sin in the knowledge that it's already forgiven anyway. As you can see, we are smack dab where we started in this rather circular argument. This, then, is the dilemma that today's theologians still struggle with.

Calvin's answer was to believe that God had predetermined it all from the very beginning. Calvinism taught that God "freely and unchangeably ordained whatsoever comes to pass." From this belief, it was determined that God had preordained some to salvation by grace, while others had been preordained to be doomed to eternal damnation for all their sins. This seems to fly in the face of 2 Peter 3:9, which says, "The Lord is not slow in keeping his promise, as some understand slowness. Instead, he is patient with you, not wanting anyone to perish, but everyone to come to repentance." If salvation was all preordained, on the other hand, then what's the point of any of it?

And many—including a former Carmelite monk by the name of Jérôme Bolsec—were keen to ask that very question. Bolsec made his way to Geneva in 1551 and actively engaged with the Calvinist movement, arguing that predestination was wrong. Jérôme argued that it was so wrong, in fact, that such belief rendered a just and holy God as the author of both good and evil. Jérôme Bolsec believed that such a treacherously unstable house of cards simply could not stand.

It was Jesus himself, after all, who refuted such a notion. According to Scripture, when unbelievers accused Christ of casting out devils through the work of devils, Christ famously stated that "if a house be divided against itself, that house cannot stand." Bolsec similarly argued that there was no way God would predetermine damnation. What was the response to Bolsec's carefully crafted argument? He was put in jail for blasphemy and heresy, and, upon his release, told to not come back.

As you can see, the sad irony all throughout the Protestant Reformation is the fact that once the previously persecuted reformers gained enough power, they in turn were ready to actively persecute others. The Calvinists, likewise, were not at all opposed to dishing out punishment to those whose beliefs they disagreed with.

Bolsec became understandably disillusioned with the Reformation after his experiences with the Calvinists—so much so that he returned to the Catholic Church. He later published a book about John Calvin in 1577 in which he blasted the reformer, calling him "a man among all others who were ever in the world ambitious, presumptuous, arrogant, cruel, malicious, vengeful, and above all ignorant." But if Bolsec thought he had been treated harshly by the Calvinists, it was nothing compared to what happened to a visiting Spaniard by the name of Miguel Servetus.

Miguel was a doctor by trade but had gotten himself into controversy by questioning the trinity, claiming that the notion was not biblical and had been completely contrived. He wrote a book that expounded upon his belief called *Restitutio*, which was published in 1553. Since most Protestants then believed in the trinity, Miguel managed to anger both trinity-believing Catholics and trinity-believing Protestants in just about equal measure.

Consequently, Miguel became a fugitive and was on the run when he decided to pass through Geneva, Switzerland. It was here that Miguel—now an infamous figure—was accosted by the Protestants. He was subsequently tried in Geneva for heresy, and on October 27, 1553, he was found guilty and sentenced to be burned at the stake. Calvin, who had previously expressed his extreme revulsion to Miguel's beliefs, tried to intervene on his behalf and lessen the severity of his execution by requesting he be decapitated instead of being burned alive.

But even this courtesy was not allowed, and Miguel was burned at the stake as planned. Even though Calvin was the one showing some restraint, Miguel's death was later blamed on him. And, while some came to view Miguel as a martyr, they also began to see Calvin as a tyrant. At the theological level, another opponent to Calvin was the French thinker Sebastian Castellio, to whom all the talk about predestination, free will, angels, and the like was pointless when all that truly mattered was faith in Christ.

Sebastian Castellio argued that doctrine was imprecise, people were imperfect, and we would never be able to understand everything correctly. Having that said, Castellio contended that believers shouldn't worry so much about the correct interpretation of Scripture but simply believe as best they can, just as the "tax collectors and prostitutes" did in the New Testament. Castellio also came to the wise conclusion that there was no point in punishing heresy since no one could agree on just what might be heretical.

As Sebastian Castellio put it, "There is hardly one of all the sects, which today are without number, which does not hold the others to be heretics. So that if in one city or region you are esteemed a true believer, in the next you will be esteemed a heretic. So that if anyone today wants to live, he must have as many faiths and religions as there are cities or sects, just as a man who travels through the lands has to change his money from day to day."

Castellio, an astute and shrewd observer of what was happening around him, could see how ridiculous it was that an interpretation of Scripture that was esteemed in one city could just as easily earn one the death penalty in another. This was obviously not a sustainable model for human religious practice. Castellio had come to believe that a more general human decency was better than a zealous striving toward doctrinal correctness.

In this regard, Castellio declared, "It would be better to let a hundred, even a thousand heretics live than to put a decent man to death under pretense of heresy." Sebastian Castellio was in many ways ahead of his time with his advanced humanistic views. But as much as such statements might seem reasonable to most of us today, they provoked quite a bit of wrath in his own time. Swiss Protestants were enraged by his words—irked at the notion that he would seek to diminish biblical truth.

One Swiss reformer, Theodore de Beze, even went so far as to charge that Sebastian Castellio "advises everyone to believe whatever he wants, opening the door by this means to all heresies and false doctrines." As hard as it is for us to fathom today, many hardline Catholics and Protestants both held to their beliefs so strongly that they were willing to both die and kill for them if need be.

Calvin himself was not swayed by such arguments for religious tolerance, and in 1554 wrote up a treatise on the trinity, in which— among other things—he argued that the execution of heretics such as Miguel Servetus was completely justifiable. He continued to consolidate his power over the next few years, and in June of 1559, he established a Bible college in which his beliefs could be routinely taught in their most precise form. It was from these Calvinist missionaries that John Calvin would export his brand of the Reformation abroad.

Chapter 9 – England Rolls Back Reformation

"What made Luther's stance so outrageous was not that he valorized the Bible. That is hardly unusual for Christians. What was shocking was that he set it above everything else. He treated the views of the early church fathers, of more recent scholars, even of church councils, with great respect, but he would not be constrained by them. In the end, anything outside the Bible, including anyone else's interpretation of the Bible, was a mere opinion. This was true and enduring radicalism of Protestantism: it's readiness to question every human authority and tradition."

- Alec Ryrie

After King Henry VIII passed away in January of 1547, the state of religion—or perhaps even better put, the state religion—of England had become entrenched in uncertainty. It was Henry VIII who had launched a pseudo-reformation in which he basically created his own state version of Catholicism, with himself at the head as both religious and political statesman. This meant that upon his death, this unique role would be given to his successor—the king's son, Edward VI.

King Henry's heir was only nine years old at the time of his passing, however, and was certainly not ready to perform as the sovereign political and religious monarch of England. Stepping into that role until Edward VI was ready to rule was Edward VI's uncle—also named Edward—Edward Seymour, the Duke of Somerset. The Duke of Somerset was given great power as the Lord Protector while Edward VI remained in his minority.

In the meantime, the Protestant world looked toward both King Edward VI and the Duke of Somerset with hope for future reform. Even John Calvin sent his best wishes from Geneva, telling the Duke of Somerset, "This is the age of salvation when God's word has been revealed." And these hopes were not unfounded. The earliest sign of reform came in July 1547, when the new royal government began to issue sweeping reforms in how church services were administered.

Of primary concern were traditional objects that had been largely associated with Catholicism, such as holy water, palm crosses, and the like. These were done away with, as well as many other religious icons. Along with these reformatory efforts, it was mandated that church clergy read a government-backed homily—or religious discourse—to their congregations during church services. The homily was a standard part of Catholic mass, but even though this tradition was kept, it was reformed to adhere to certain standards set by the government.

Another major change was enacted with the ending of the so-called chantries. These consisted of priests who sang and chanted prayers for the dearly departed believed to be in purgatory. Here, the Church of England had come to an agreement with many other reformers and decided that they would also disavow the concept of purgatory. It was declared that such things were not necessary and only took away from the perfect salvation through the death of Jesus Christ.

But perhaps the most important reform occurred in 1549 with the Act of Uniformity. This regulation saw to it that the Latin mass was replaced by the specially-created English-based liturgy known as the *Book of Common Prayer*, established by the Archbishop of Canterbury, Cranmer. This universal decree was carried out in force with the sole exception of the universities of Cambridge and Oxford, where allowances were made for scholars to still be permitted to say their prayers in the Latin tongue.

The Archbishop of Canterbury had placed a powerfully written essay inside the *Book of Common Prayer*, which served to set the tone for this moment in the English Reformation. The essay was called "Of Ceremonies: Why Some Be Abolished and Some Retained." As one might imagine, the subject matter covered why some of the previous religious customs had been done away with while others were kept in place. In the text, Cranmer spoke of how previous religious rituals had "blinded the people and obscured the glory of God."

It was for the sake of clarity, then, that the old ceremonial practices had to be put aside. But as much as the archbishop tried to sell the change as being for the church's own good, not everyone agreed. In the towns of Cornwall and Devon, an all-out rebellion was ignited by outraged parishioners who demanded that their old customs be restored. Known as the Western Rebellion, this episode involved infuriated churchgoers taking the prayer books and setting them ablaze.

These protesters of this seemingly homegrown Protestant Reformation then went to the administrative district of Exeter, where they made their demands known. Among them was a call to bring back Henry VIII's previous ban of English-translated Bibles. They also sought to bring back icons that were used to pray for loved ones believed to be in purgatory. They wanted to do all these things "just as [their] forefathers did."

Many of the Christian laity in these days were in the habit of reciting memorized Latin Scripture and prayers even though they did not always understand the words they were reciting. It was a pure muscle memory exercise they repeated by ear—just as their forefathers before them had done. Archbishop Cranmer took issue with this and criticized the dissidents by arguing that reciting Latin words that they did not clearly understand was no better than being a parrot.

In the end, the dissidents were only brought down by force, and after royal troops arrived from London, a violent melee ensued, killing many of the protestors. The leaders of the protest were also seized, and many of them received the death penalty for their actions. King Edward's Lord Protector, the Duke of Somerset, was having some problems of his own, meanwhile. He had been leading battles against both Scotland and France, and with the addition of having to put down insurrections at home, England was going broke.

Discontent with his leadership led to plotting against him that culminated with the Earl of Warwick taking over. The Earl of Warwick received the title of "Lord President" in the spring of 1550, and thereafter would call the shots. Soon after this power grab, Archbishop Cranmer decided to enact even more religious reform by restructuring the role of the priest. Rather than hold a primary duty of administering sacraments, the priest was made to serve more of a pastoral function and expected to focus on preaching the gospel to church members instead.

As reformative as the *Book of Common Prayer* was, its own author—the Archbishop of Canterbury—had begun to think that it was lacking. One of the problems was the fact that much of the previous Catholic language about mass had remained intact. Cranmer wanted to distance himself from such things, so he crafted a revised edition of the prayer book in 1552 in which he carefully removed terms such as "mass" and replaced them with "Lord's Supper" or "holy communion."

But, as is usually the case, Archbishop Cranmer still had his critics. One of his more vocal critics was John Knox, a royal chaplain who found the prayer book's admonition to kneel during communion to be unbiblical. After all, during Christ's last supper in the New Testament in which he ate and drank with the disciples—upon which communion is based—there was no one kneeling. Rather than taking the criticism seriously, however, Archbishop Cranmer refused to listen to such critiques and castigated such opponents as merely "unquiet spirits."

To further distance the Church of England from the Catholic Church, the revised prayer book also contained the Forty-Two Articles, which highlighted the main differences between the two. Specifically, Cranmer claimed that purgatory, indulgences, the veneration of images and relics, and the invocation of saints were not scriptural. The Archbishop of Canterbury denounced these Catholic beliefs and practices as "a fond thing vainly invented, and ground upon no warrant of Scripture."

But as any good Catholic knows, this is not entirely true. Both the belief of purgatory and the practice of indulgences, for example, are indeed based on Scripture. It's not something a priest simply made up out of thin air. The notions are gleaned largely from the book of Maccabees, a so-called apocryphal text that Protestants such as Martin Luther decided to omit from all Protestant copies of the Bible.

It would be one thing to disagree with the Catholic Church's interpretation of the Bible, but to say that such things are not based on Scripture is a bending of reality to suit Protestant ends. At any rate, the Archbishop of Canterbury seemed to have a free hand in both interpreting Scripture and reforming the church for a time, and for the most part did as he pleased. The momentum for reform, however, would come to a halt on July 6, 1553, when word was received that the young King Edward had passed away.

It's interesting to note that the monumental efforts that his father Henry VIII made to bring a son into this world seemingly came to naught. Henry VIII had largely broken Catholic Church tradition just to put away one wife and gain another that could bear him a son. But six wives later and an English Reformation partially underway, the main purpose of all the deceased king's efforts had perished along with him.

The death of King Edward sent shockwaves through the kingdom. But as is almost always the case in dynastic royal families, there was a back-up plan. According to Henry's will, in the event of his son's death, the crown would be handed over to Edward's eldest sister—Princess Mary. This Mary was the daughter of the Katherine of Aragon—Henry's first wife, whose marriage he had annulled and quietly put away. Ironically, Henry had left Katherine in search of a wife who would give him a son to avoid his throne being given to his and Katherine's daughter Mary. Yet, that is precisely what occurred.

Mary, who had lived through all the recent somersaults in English theology, was a diehard Catholic who very much wished to turn the clock back on England's recent Reformation. Those in government knew that this would be the case and, in a last-ditch effort, tried to thwart the queen's rise to power by backing the Protestant daughter of the Duke of Suffolk—Lady Jane Grey—instead. But as much as those who leaned Protestant rose against her, Mary successfully shored up support from those sympathetic to Catholicism.

Holed up in Framlingham Castle in Suffolk, the queen rallied her supporters around her, and in the face of her fierce support, her challengers decided to give up the fight, allowing Mary to retain the throne. Initially, Mary had hinted to her court that she intended to practice a wide-ranging religious tolerance. But soon into her reign, this proved to be more lip service than anything else. For once her power had been consolidated and assured, the queen went on a rampage. She had all Protestant preaching licenses revoked and had prominent Protestants arrested.

In this sudden role reversal, she then made sure that Catholic priests that had been imprisoned under her brother Edward VI were released and placed back in charge of their parishes. By the end of the year, all the new religious literature—including the Archbishop's *Book of Common Prayer*—were removed from circulation, and the traditional Catholic mass was back in place. England had seemingly reverted to Catholicism in just a matter of months.

Even more distressing to the Protestants was the news that Queen Mary was planning to marry Philip II of Spain—the son of the Holy Roman Emperor, Charles V. This marriage of political convenience had been hatched by Emperor Charles himself, who sought to wed his son with the new Catholic Queen of England to ensure both political and religious stability in the region. Fearing that their nation would become subsumed by the Holy Roman Empire due to such a union, many in the British Parliament predictably objected to the union.

It was for this reason that Queen Mary—in what was perhaps not the most eloquent of phraseology—was petitioned by the House of Commons not to wed a foreigner. Once it was clear that the queen would not be persuaded by Parliament, a noble by the name of Sir Thomas Wyatt attempted an outright coup by sending an army of some 3,000 to descend upon the queen in London. The queen's forces were more than capable of defending their monarch, however, and the army was repulsed. In the melee, Sir Thomas Wyatt was captured and summarily executed. Queen Mary was going to become the wife of Spain's King Philip whether anyone liked it or not, and the two were duly wed on July 25, 1554.

Previous reformers, such as Archbishop of Canterbury Thomas Cranmer, meanwhile were being arrested and put on trial with sudden demands for them to denounce their non-Catholic beliefs. For all intents and purposes, before the year was out, the pope was ready to welcome England back to the Roman Catholic fold with open arms. And on November 30, 1554, it was made official—England had returned to the Mother Church.

With England back in the Catholic embrace, it wasn't long before the power of the Catholic faction began to ramp up persecution of those who dared to remain Protestant. Aiding them in this was a decision by Mary's government, made in January of 1555, to implement traditional Catholic heresy laws through the old Catholic standard "On the Burning of Heretics." As the name implies, these laws gave license to the lethal punishment of any so much as accused of being heretical.

This led to several high-profile heresy trials, which amounted to nothing more than show trials reminiscent of Martin Luther's interrogation at the Diet of Worms. The main goal of such occasions was to prove Protestants to be in error while reinforcing Catholic supremacy. They also served to set examples for others lest they decide to go the same way as other supposed heretics. One of the first to be killed in this great purge was a popular London pastor by the name of John Rogers.

Rogers was burned at the stake for his refusal to submit to Catholic doctrine. Even as they lit the flames, John Rogers had steadfastly proclaimed, "That which I have preached I will seal with my blood." His death was followed by many others, and by late 1558, it's said that some 280 men and women were killed, along with countless others who simply perished while behind bars. The persecution was so bad that, at one point, even an infant who was born to a condemned woman was burned at the stake right alongside his mother.

This was apparently too much even for the most bloodthirsty of Catholic zealots, however, and the sheriff who made the fateful decision to burn the baby was ultimately charged and found guilty of homicide for the transgression. The man who had been the architect behind much of England's Protestant reform in the meantime— Archbishop Thomas Cranmer—had been arrested and kept under lock and key. In this cell, he was isolated and routinely interrogated by those who held him.

After these repeated rounds of questioning, he finally snapped and found himself signing his recantation in 1556. This led to another more formal recantation, and Cranmer officially acquiescing to papal power.

But the recantation did not last. Archbishop Cranmer was taken to Oxford University on March 21, 1556, to speak before those assembled as to why he came back to the Catholic faith. Cranmer surprised them all, however, when he began to denounce not his previous reforms but the Catholic Church and his recantation. His denunciation ended with "and as for the pope, I refuse him as Christ's enemy and false doctrine."

This was obviously not at all what the Catholic faithful wanted to hear. Once his handlers got over their shock, they immediately seized Archbishop Cranmer and proceeded to haul him off to an execution site in which he could be burned to death. It is said that while Archbishop Cranmer went up in flames, he quoted from Scripture. He repeated the words Saint Stephen had uttered while being stoned. Cranmer cried, "Lord Jesus, receive my spirit! I see the heavens open and Jesus standing at the right hand of God!"

With one of the chief architects of England's Reformation burned at the stake, it seemed that the cause for the Protestant Reformation in England was all but lost. But then, on November 17, 1558, the unexpected happened. Queen Mary died. She was only forty-two years old, but as it turns out, she had a terminal case of stomach cancer. So ended the reign of the queen who would be forever remembered as "Bloody Mary."

She was put down not by an armed overthrow from without but by cancerous tumors from within. Upon her death, Princess Elizabeth took the throne. Elizabeth was a supporter of the Reformation, and as soon as she came to power, she reversed course, broke with the Catholic Church, and began to restore the gains that had been made in England's long, drawn-out march toward religious reformation.

Chapter 10 – Huguenots, the Netherlands, and William of Orange

"In running over the pages of our history for seven hundred years, we shall scarcely find a single great event which has not promoted equality of condition. The Crusades and the English wars decimated the nobles and divided their possessions. The municipal corporations introduced democratic liberty into the bosom of feudal monarchy. The invention of fire-arms equalized the vassal and the noble on the field of battle. The art of printing opened the same resources to the minds of all classes. The post office brought knowledge alike to the door of the cottage and to the gate of the palace. And Protestantism proclaimed that all men are alike and able to find the road to heaven. The discovery of America opened a thousand new paths to fortune, and led obscure adventurers to wealth and power."

- Alexis de Tocqueville

The Huguenots were Protestants who were influenced by Calvinist beliefs who took root in southwestern France in the 16th Century. Since France was officially Catholic at the time, the Huguenots had to meet in secret. They did this through a network of many Huguenot safe houses scattered throughout France. Geneva, meanwhile, remained the spiritual capital of these French reformers—and Calvinist writings were routinely smuggled into the Huguenot domain.

All this activity was, of course, vigorously rejected by French governance. In 1547, the king of France, Henri II, created a commission called "the burning chamber" specifically charged with the task of rooting out supposed heretical movements like the Huguenots. If the name doesn't give it away, the burning chamber was certainly not above killing heretics by burning them at the stake.

In fact, during the first few years of the commission, it is said that thirty-nine reformers were executed by fire or hanging. It was shortly after this purge that the Edict of Châteaubriant was issued in June of 1551. This edict enabled lower courts to have the power to carry out the execution of presumed heretics without so much as even consulting the parliamentary government.

Meanwhile over in Geneva, John Calvin—whom most Huguenots viewed as their spiritual leader, looked at these moves as nothing short of draconian. Even though Calvin also had heretics condemned, he at least gave them some semblance of a trial (although it's certainly debatable how fair they were). At any rate, for a time, France seemed to corner the market on routine execution of religious dissidents during this period.

Much of this persecution of the Huguenots was covered in Jean Crespin's 1554 text, *Le Livre des Martyrs*. In it, Crespin documented quite well how those punished were rounded up, tortured, and executed. To make matters even more disturbing, often the tongues of the martyrs were removed beforehand to keep them from professing their faith to the crowd. They were denied even the chance to give their last testament to those who were persecuting them.

There would be no last words—these oppressed souls had to burn in silence. In the fall of 1557, John Calvin attempted to encourage the French faithful, issuing a statement that read in part, "God desires to try our faith, like gold in the furnace—yet he fails not to treasure up their precious tears." The encouragement must have helped because, by 1559, it was clear that despite their persecution, the Huguenot movement was growing.

That spring, a group of some thirty different parishes met in France to pledge their allegiance to Calvinist doctrine. John Calvin also began to send his missionary pastors, who were trained at his Geneva Academy, to France to spread Calvinist beliefs even further. It's said that by 1564, some 100 of these Calvinist missionaries had been sent. And it seemed that all these efforts were indeed making a difference—most notably by way of the impressive rate at which members of the French upper classes began to embrace the faith.

It was amidst this renewed sympathy towards the reformers among French nobility that King Henri II unexpectedly perished during a friendly game of jousting. It was a complete accident. The elder Henri had been jousting with the younger Gabriel comte de Montgomery in celebration of his daughter's impending wedding. In their last round of jousting, Gabriel lifted his lance, charged, and accidentally struck the king head-on, causing his lance to shatter and break. It was one of the shards from his broken lance that tore through the gaps in the king's visor, slicing through the king's eye and lodging into his brain.

Interestingly, the French mystic Michel de Nostradamus has long been credited with predicting this tragedy. A few years prior, Nostradamus had published a book of vaguely-worded quatrains that allegedly predict future events, and one of them is said to have been written about this event. The quatrain stated, "The young lion will overcome the older one / On the field of combat in a single battle; He will pierce his eyes through a golden cage, / Two wounds made one, then he dies a cruel death."

Henri did indeed die a cruel death in terrible pain, perishing from the mortal wound days after the fact. In the prediction, the old lion is said to be Henri and the young lion Gabriel, who pierced Henri's eyes through his "golden cage"—in other words, pierced his eyes through his protective, cage-like visor. Nevertheless, the jury is still out on whether Nostradamus truly predicted this event or just got incredibly lucky. At any rate, it was after his death that King Henri II's successor Francois II began to renew persecution of the Huguenots.

To end the onslaught, a group of Huguenots attempted to forcibly seize the new king and hold him hostage in the spring of 1560. But their plot was found out before it could be implemented, and the plotters were apprehended. Among those who participated in the scheme were quite a few of the missionary pastors sent over from Geneva, Switzerland.

As it turns out, the plotters wasted a lot of time and energy on a problem that was on the verge of solving itself. For, in December of that very year, the young French King Francois II suddenly perished—not from the blade of an assassin, but by way of a dreadful ear infection. Upon Francois II's death, the scepter of power was handed to his brother, King Charles IX—but, since his brother was only ten years old at the time, his mother Catherine de Medici would rule in his stead until the boy king came of age.

Catherine de Medici proved to be a pragmatic politician. Sensing that her position was rather precarious, she reached out to the Huguenots to use them as a bargaining chip and wedge against the other factions arrayed against her. Also sensing that the country could not go on without some sort of compromise between the Protestants and Catholics, Catherine made a genuine effort to bridge the divide.

In furtherance of this goal, she held a summit in the fall of 1561 in which representatives of the Catholics and Protestant reformers met and openly discussed their doctrinal differences. It was a rare moment of open-minded engagement in which opposing sides could speak about their differing opinions rather than immediately slaughtering each other over them.

The meeting itself did not seem to bring much agreement, but nevertheless, in January of 1562, Huguenots were finally granted some degree of tolerance. In the Edict of St. Germain-en-Laye, it was determined that the Huguenots would be allowed to practice their faith without fear of prosecution, providing they held their gatherings outside towns, unarmed, by day, and under supervision.

Unfortunately, the toleration did not last very long at all. In March of 1562, a group of Huguenots was confronted at one of their gatherings, and the unarmed members of the flock were assaulted. The Huguenots were following the regulations as given to them—simply meeting at a barn right outside the city limits of Vassy, France—when Francis, Duke of Guise, unleashed his forces upon them. Francis later tried to claim that he did not order the attack but that it was a spontaneous violent reaction after Huguenots threw stones at his men.

At any rate, this attack left about seventy Huguenots dead and kicked off a back and forth spate of violence that would continue over the next several years. The worst eruption of this violence occurred in 1572 during the so-called St. Bartholomew's Day Massacre. The killing began on August 23, 1572, and continued for three days as militant Catholic groups systemically killed tens of thousands of Huguenots. Historians still debate the cause of the violence, whether it was spontaneous or engineered by a French official such as the Catholic Queen Catherine de Medici.

The massacre erupted following a week of festivity in France. King Charles IX was hosting the marital ceremony of Prince Henri of Navarre and his sister Margaret. Navarre was a Protestant prince, and his marriage to the Catholic Margaret was seen as a means to bring some sort of unity between Catholics and Protestants in France. Sadly, such things were not to be, and shortly after this week of feasting, the massacre occurred.

Initially, it was French troops who attacked the Huguenots, but soon Catholic civilians began to join in—literally going door to door seeking Huguenots to kill. Whatever the cause may have been, this latest Huguenot slaughter convinced many that living in France had become impossible and led to an exodus of many Huguenots to safer ground in England, Germany, and the Netherlands. Of these locales, the Netherlands would host the next major showdown between the forces of Catholicism and Protestantism.

Ever since Holy Roman Emperor Charles V had stepped down in 1556 and handed over power to his brother Ferdinand, it was agreed that direct control of what was then known as the Low Countries, or the Netherlands—which today would constitute modern-day Holland, Belgium, Luxemburg, and a piece of northern France—would fall under the dominion of the outgoing emperor's son, Philip II of Spain. Philip was too preoccupied with matters in Spain, however, and in 1559, he opted to grant his half-sister, Margaret of Parma, the authority to call the shots in this region instead.

Philip II was a staunch Catholic, but in his absence, the leading nobility of the Netherlands began to show their true colors as it pertained to support of Protestant movements and to personally back certain leaders and flocks associated with the Reformation. Philip was not too pleased by this, and as soon as he heard of it, he demanded that all supposed heresy be rooted out from the realm immediately. Nevertheless, the upper classes of the Netherlands continued to flirt with those Philip called heretics. In the meantime, a Dutch reformer by the name of Hendrik van Brederode launched the so-called League of Compromise in the fall of 1565. All of this was done to roll back restrictions that had been placed upon reformers.

When change wasn't forthcoming enough, the reformers upped the ante considerably by taking their case to Margaret of Parma. After they pressured Margaret with the specter of massive unrest unless she acted, she tried to curtail the persecution of Protestants. It was now clear that Margaret of Parma was playing a weak hand, and Protestants took advantage of it, holding massive rallies and speaking engagements in which Calvinist doctrine was freely discussed.

As was all too often the case during the Reformation, as the Protestants grew bolder, this previously persecuted group of believers soon became the ones doing the persecuting. The Protestants were against any form of religious icon or relic Catholics revered and began to strike out at Catholic Churches, tearing down paintings, sculptures, ritual implements, and the like. They also burned any Catholic literature they came across.

These Protestants wanted to be tolerated just long enough to show how intolerable they themselves could be, it seems. Their behavior shouldn't be all that surprising considering that the source of their doctrine—John Calvin—was well known for his religious intolerance. Calvin had many tortured and killed simply for having beliefs contrary to his own, as was most famously seen in the death of Miguel Servetus.

Even though it certainly wasn't a happy time for Catholics who were being assaulted and witnessing their churches demolished, it was a wonderful time for the Protestant reformers. In fact, they would later recall the year 1566 as the "Wonder Year." Margaret of Parma, meanwhile, was recalled, and the Duke of Alba was placed in charge of affairs in the Netherlands. The Duke of Alba arrived in the summer of 1567 at the head of a massive number of troops.

With the arrival of the Duke of Alba, the tables were once again decisively turned, and the persecution of Protestants began anew. The duke set up his infamous Council of Blood, in which about 10,000 were tried for heresy and at least 1,000 received the death penalty. This kicked off yet another exodus of Huguenots and other Protestants—fleeing for the high ground of German, Swiss, and English lands. In the meantime, the movement's leader, Brederode, passed away in the spring of 1568, leading to a vacuum in stewardship.

Stepping into the void was Prince William I—or, as he was more widely known, Prince William of Orange. He was called this because he controlled The Principality of Orange, which in those days consisted of part of southern France. William of Orange was a member of the Catholic nobility and had previously been neutral in the conflict, but after becoming increasingly dissatisfied with Spanish oppression of local estates and the persecution of reformers, he decided to throw in his lot with the Protestants.

William of Orange led an army against Alba's troops in 1568 but was defeated. He persisted, however, and continued a protracted kind of guerrilla warfare that would eventually lead to a major rebellion in 1572. Aiding the Protestant cause was the great discontent that Alba had created in the general population by enforcing draconian taxation on the masses. In a similar way to how Martin Luther stoked local resentment against foreign Catholic interference from Rome, William of Orange tapped into the same kind of suspicion in his subjects when it came to their Spanish Catholic overlords.

The popular uprising came to a climax when a group of pirates known as "Sea Beggars" managed to capture the port of Brill and lay siege to settlements all along the coastline. Then that August, right around the time of the infamous St. Bartholomew's Day massacre that had killed so many Huguenots in France, William of Orange took an army of tens of thousands of troops and stormed into Brabant—a part of modern-day Belgium. This assault was soon copied by several other rebel reformers.

Being attacked by both land and sea, the Duke of Alba tried to come back hard at the rebels, massacring whole towns that were in his path. His onslaught stopped the Protestants in the south, but in the northern regions, the struggle continued. It was easier to put up a resistance in the north due to both its political makeup and its geography. The north had much less of a homegrown Catholic base, and the physical terrain, with rivers and frequent flooding, was simply much more difficult for Catholic troops to invade.

Stuck in a perpetual stalemate, this long, drawn-out conflict ended up literally dividing the Netherlands along ideological lines. Ultimately, the southern region agreed to sign the Union of Arras, maintaining that they would hold fast to the Catholic Church and Spanish dominion. In the north, however, Calvinism still reigned supreme, and this led the reformers to strike up their own union, the

Union of Utrecht, which was basically a pact of self-defense among the reformers in the event of foreign invasion.

By 1580, meanwhile, the Duke of Alba was out of the picture, replaced by the Duke of Parma—Alessandro Farnese. The Duke of Parma proved himself to be much more formidable in the field of battle than the Duke of Alba had been and managed to claw back Antwerp, Ghent, and Brussels from the rebels in rapid succession.

At the same time, back in Spain, Philip II made sure that William of Orange was a marked man. He castigated him as "the chief disturber of the whole state of Christendom" and extolled all good Catholics "to do him injury or take him from this world as a public enemy." Along with these words of encouragement to any would-be assassins, King Philip also placed a big bounty on the Prince of Orange, promising financial gain for anyone who was willing to take him out. The Prince of Orange was now literally a hunted man.

The first to corner their quarry was Juan de Jáuregui—a simple Spanish merchant—who came upon the prince in 1582 and managed to shoot him in both the neck and head. The Prince of Orange would miraculously survive these injuries, but it wasn't long before he faced off with another assailant hell-bent on fulfilling Philip II's directive. In July of 1584, Orange was tracked down by a lowly cabinet maker's apprentice named Balthasar Gérard.

This man managed to gain access to where the Prince of Orange was staying and then simply walked right up to him and opened fire. William was hit multiple times in the chest and abdomen. It is said that as the Prince of Orange crumpled to the ground, he shouted, "My God, have mercy on my soul!" followed by "My God, have mercy on this poor people!" Meanwhile, the assassin tried to flee, but the prince's enraged followers easily subdued him.

Gérard was not going to get away with such a brazen act and would suffer greatly for what he had done—tortured and killed by the vengeful followers of the Prince of Orange. Even though Gérard couldn't cash in on the murder, his parents were paid in full by King Philip. The death of the Prince of Orange brought immediate confusion as to how the reform movement in the Netherlands could go forward.

William of Orange's son Maurice attempted to take up the mantle of his father. Many, however, feared that it was all about to fall apart. But the reforms received some surprising aid in the summer of 1585 when Queen Elizabeth I of England sent troops to shore up the rebel reformer's strength. The queen also signed the Treaty of Nonsuch, a document that pledged intervention if the Netherlands faced invasion.

There are a few reasons why Queen Elizabeth would do this. Spain was, at this point, a political, military, and religious rival of the reformed English, and it was in the best interest of the British to have an allied (or at least neutral) Protestant buffer zone in the Netherlands. This act prevented Spanish invasion and secured the Dutch Protestants of the Netherlands, which would eventually become the Dutch Republic, where the beliefs of the Protestant Reformation would not only be tolerated but also flourish.

The victory of the Netherlands over Catholic dominion was one of the greatest success stories of the Protestant Reformation. Many of the reformers based in the Netherlands would travel far and wide, spreading the gospel of their beliefs and way of life. Some traveled all the way to the United States of America, where they set up successful enclaves that are still in existence today.

Conclusion: How the Reformation Changed the World

When Martin Luther nailed his Ninety-five Theses to the doors of Wittenberg University, he set off a series of consequences that would have been impossible for him to have predicted. Luther had opened the door for debate, and suddenly there were protesters on every corner asking questions about why Roman Catholic doctrine was the way it was. These protesters of the religious mainstream—or, as we know them today, these Protestants—dared to hold the religious authorities of their day to task.

They wondered if purgatory was real, if faith without works would be sufficient, and if it was truly possible—or even appropriate—to pray for the dead. And when their Catholic minders failed to provide them with adequate answers to their questions, it only spurred them to ask even more. This, of course, led to the inevitable backlash of the Catholic Church persecuting the sects that arose in opposition to official Church doctrine. Unlike times past when dissidents would rise up only to be quickly cast aside, by the time Marin Luther came to prominence, these Protestants of the faith were hard for the Mother Church to shake off.

They also had a powerful tool at their disposal by way of the printing press. As Protestants printed off religious tract after religious tract, they were ensuring that their interpretation of Scripture would last long after they themselves were gone. The Catholic Church needed to come to the realization that, although they could kill the Protestant Reformers themselves, they could not kill their ideas. And as the power base of the Protestants grew, they began to govern their own cities and even countries where, for a change, they could call the shots regarding religious beliefs.

Sadly, when Protestants were finally free of persecution and able to practice as they pleased, they often turned into persecutors themselves. John Calvin, after all, burned those with differing beliefs just as fervently as the Catholics would have burned him. As much as the Reformation was an explosion of the freedom of thought and religion, it also produced dogmatic sects—so dogmatic, in fact, that each jealously guarded their form of religious expression and were willing to destroy anyone else who dared to see things from another perspective.

Although great good came from the Reformation, this was the great tragedy of the Protestants. They despised the Catholics for forcing their interpretation of Scriptures on the masses, yet they were more than ready to turn around and try to force their own heavy-handed views on others. Yes, history does indeed repeat itself, and the course of the Reformation demonstrated this phenomenon in a startling and dramatic fashion.

But, despite the perpetual back and forth rounds of persecution on both sides, much good came from the Reformation. It was the freedom of thought fostered by the Reformation, after all, that led to that other period of revolution in thinking—the Renaissance. Although the Reformation was a religious movement in nature, for many it seemed to settle some pretty serious philosophical arguments beneficial to the Renaissance.

For one thing, the Protestants defied the idea that the pope or priests had any special authority above anyone else. The Protestants took to heart Galatians 3:28, in which the Apostle Paul declared, "There is neither Jew nor Gentile, neither slave nor free, nor is there male and female, for you are all one in Christ Jesus." The acceptance of these words led to the widespread belief that all were equal under God. This leveling of the playing field worked as a bulldozer, upending the medieval belief in a natural hierarchy of authority.

Even if you didn't believe in God, the idea that everyone was equal was an eye-opening proclamation, and it was the Reformation that brought these notions directly to the masses. Protestants also encouraged innovation and a strong work ethic—all things that would find their way from Europe to a place called America. It was in America that the real fruits of the Reformation blossomed.

Free of any idea of social or religious hierarchy, the good folks of America worked hard and tried to live a good life. Following their religious precepts, they knew that hard work and a little bit of faith were all that truly mattered. The industrious free enterprise inspired by the Protestant Reformation is still bearing fruit in the United States of America to this day.

The Reformation was many things to many people, but above all, it was the seminal moment that changed the trajectory of the world for good.

Here's another book by Captivating History that you might like

Free Bonus from Captivating History (Available for a Limited time)

Hi History Lovers!

Now you have a chance to join our exclusive history list so you can get your first history ebook for free as well as discounts and a potential to get more history books for free! Simply visit the link below to join.

Captivatinghistory.com/ebook

Also, make sure to follow us on Facebook, Twitter and Youtube by searching for Captivating History.

Appendix A: Further Reading and Reference

Reformation: A World in Turmoil. Andrew Atherstone

The Origins and Developments of the Dutch Revolt. Graham Darby

Martin Luther: A Biography for the People. Dyron B. Daughrity

Made in United States
Troutdale, OR
08/23/2023

12315732R00056